# Actions with Fractions

**Author**
Dr. Arthur J. Wiebe

**Editor**
Betty Cordel

**Illustrator**
Reneé Mason

**Desktop Publisher**
Kristy Shuler

# Actions with Fractions

## Table of Contents

# Actions with Fractions

The activities in *Actions with Fractions* are designed to provide multiple experiences that address the *NCTM Standards* listed on page iv. The emphasis on the development of fraction number sense is crucial to building success in operations involving fractions. The interrelationship of fractions, decimals, percents, ratios, and proportions is the special focus of activities which involve graphing on the coordinate plane.

It is the intent of this resource to provide teachers with a broad selection of activities with the expectation that they will select and order activities for insertion into their mathematics program as appropriate. For this purpose the objective rather than the order of activities selected is important. Activities are equally useful for initial instruction, review, or assessment.

## Building the Foundation for the Study of Fractions

The foundation for a successful and meaningful study of fractions is laid by **mastering** and **internalizing** four essentials:

- **the concept of fair shares**
- **the ability to recognize fractional parts in the real world, models, and representational forms**
- **an understanding of the symbolic notation for expressing fractions, and**
- **the ability to recognize, name, and use equivalent fractions.**

## The Concept of Fair Shares

Fortunately, students begin school with an intuitive understanding of fair shares. Our task is twofold: to help them understand that fractions deal exclusively with fair shares and to refine and enrich that meaning. In the symbolic representation of fractions, the denominator indicates how many fair shares have been created out of a whole and the numerator tells us how many of those fair shares are under consideration.

## Recognizing Fractional Parts

Students need many and varied experiences with recognizing fractional parts in the real world as the basis for building a strong conceptual base and developing mental images. Many activities involving appropriate manipulatives and objects should be used to nurture understanding so that when operations with fractions are performed, students have a mental image of what is transpiring and what constitutes a realistic answer. Such mental imagery is useful in estimating the result.

In line with the recommendations in reform documents, multiple representations are utilized. Seven models are used in *Actions with Fractions*: pattern blocks, pies or clocks, unit bars, unit squares, sets of objects, egg cartons, and geoboards or coordinate graphs. Each model makes it own significant contribution to understanding.

## Expressing Fractions in Symbolic Notation

Students need to understand that in symbolic notation the numerator tells *how many* fair shares and the denominator *what kind* of fair shares are under consideration. They should gain facility in translating between models and their corresponding symbolic notations. The activities in this volume provide constant opportunity to forge this important connection.

## Recognizing and Naming Equivalent Fractions

Equivalent fractions are the parallel of equivalent ratios and equivalent ratios are the building blocks for proportions. Proportions and proportional reasoning are so pervasive in mathematics that extensive attention must be given to these concepts.

Mastery of the ability to form and identify equivalent fractions lies at the heart of the basic operations of addition and subtraction. Just as knowledge of the basic facts is essential to perform operations with whole numbers so knowledge of basic equivalent fractions is essential to perform operations with fractions. *The basic facts in the study of fractions consist of the set of common equivalent fractions. Students should be expected to instantly recognize common equivalent fractions just as they are expected to know the basic addition and multiplication facts.*

Fractions with halves, thirds, fourths, sixths, eighths, tenths, and twelfths constitute more than 95% of those the average student will encounter in real life. Therefore, those should be emphasized (as they are in this volume) and students should become thoroughly familiar with them. It is of highest importance that they acquire familiarity with this subset of fractions.

# Content of *Actions with Fractions* and its Relationship to the *AIMS Model of Mathematics*

     The *AIMS Model of Mathematics* incorporates the manipulative, representational, and abstract levels of Piaget. It differs from the Piagetian progression in that it makes provision for other sequences. Anthropologists report that in certain cultures the progression differs. Therefore, some students, particularly those from other cultures, are best served by a more flexible approach. The *AIMS Model of Mathematics* provides that flexibility. The process can begin at any level and move to other levels in any order.

     Manipulative, representational, and abstract levels are generally *interwoven* in *Actions with Fractions* activities. Instead of being linear from manipulative to representational to abstract, the sequences will vary in most of the six permutations that are possible with these three levels. An activity may begin at the abstract or representational level as readily as at the manipulative level. This is particularly appropriate given the high degree of emphasis in this publication on building mental imagery.

     Aspects of the Five Star Model that receive special emphasis in *Actions with Fractions* activities are:

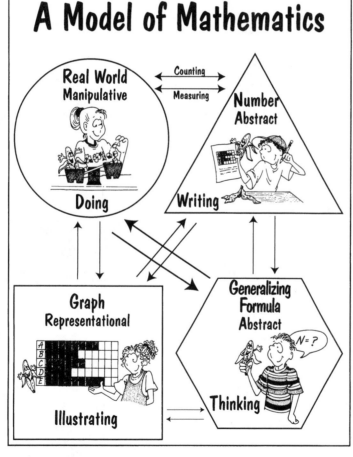

Manipulation of objects is depicted by the circle.

Pictures of fractions are represented by the square.

The triangle represents the abstract component.

The hexagon incorporates such factors as associations among the manipulative, representational, and abstract forms; the development and use of mental imagery; approximating results using mental imagery, etc.

| | |
|---|---|
| Circle: | seeing, touching, moving |
| Square: | picturing, associating pictures with manipulation and abstract notation |
| Triangle: | using abstract notation, associating notation with pictures and objects |
| Hexagon: | developing mental imagery, using mental imagery to visualize fractions, operations on fractions, and to estimate answers |

ACTIONS WITH FRACTIONS     iii     © 1998 AIMS Education Foundation

# Actions with Fractions and the NCTM Standards*

## Grades K - 4

In grades K – 4, the study of mathematics should include
  a. numerous opportunities for communication so that students can relate physical materials, pictures, and diagrams to mathematical ideas;
  b. fractions and decimals so that students can
  - develop concepts of fractions, mixed numbers, and decimals;
  - develop number sense for fractions and decimals;
  - use models to relate fractions to decimals and to find equivalent fractions;
  - use models to explore operations on fractions and decimals.

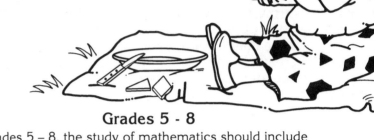

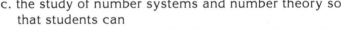

## Grades 5 - 8

In grades 5 – 8, the study of mathematics should include
  a. opportunities to communicate so that students can
  - model situations using oral, written, concrete, pictorial, graphical, and algebraic methods;
  - appreciate the value of mathematical notation and its role in the development of mathematical ideas;
  b. the continued development of number and number relationships so that students can
  - understand, represent, and use numbers in a variety of equivalent forms (integer, fraction, decimal, percent, exponential, and scientific notation) in real-world and mathematical problem situations;
  - develop number sense for whole numbers, fractions, decimals, integers, and rational numbers;
  - investigate relationships among fractions, decimals, and percents;
  - represent numerical relationships in one- and two-dimensional graphs;
  c. the study of number systems and number theory so that students can
  - understand and appreciate the need for numbers beyond the whole numbers;
  - develop and use order relationships for whole numbers, fractions, decimals, integers and rational numbers;
  - extend their understanding of whole number operations to fractions, decimals, integers, and rational numbers;
  - understand how the basic arithmetic operations are related to one another;

  d. develop the concepts underlying computation and estimation in various contexts so that students can compute with whole numbers, fractions, decimals, integers, and rational numbers.

* National Council of Teachers of Mathematics. *Curriculum and Evaluation Standards for School Mathematics.* National Council of Teachers of Mathematics, Inc. Reston, VA. 1989.

# Modeling Fractions

## Pattern Block Model

The *pattern block model* makes a significant contribution through the imprinting of strong mental images. AIMS has added fourths and twelfths pattern blocks to the traditional whole, halves, thirds, and sixths. This expanded set greatly increases the number of problem situations that can be modeled.

The strong mental impression is facilitated by the fact that the hexagon has six sides and each fraction is related to those sides in a unique manner: halves include three of the sides, thirds include two, sixths include one, fourths include one and one-half, and twelfths include one-half. Since fractions with denominators of 12 or its factors constitute the family from which most of the commonly occurring fractions are drawn, this model is worthy of extensive use. The processes of addition and subtraction of fractions are made especially meaningful with pattern block tiles.

## Pie or Clock Model

The *pie or clock model* makes several contributions. The whole is always identifiable and can be reconstructed based on the part since the part contains the radius of the circle. The functions of the numerator and denominator are differentiated. The denominator describes the shape of the part and the numerator the number of parts.

This model is useful for the addition and subtraction of fractions. Addition consists of laying sectors side by side in circular fashion as around the clock. In subtraction, the minuend is laid down first and the subtrahend is used to cover it beginning along the far side to display the difference. The uncovered part of the minuend is the difference.

Halves, thirds, fourths, sixths, and twelfths and their addition or subtraction are readily associated with a 12-hour clock. Eighths are added when a 24-hour clock is used.

The pie model illustration below shows the addition of $\frac{1}{2} + \frac{1}{3}$ and the subtraction of $\frac{1}{2} - \frac{1}{3}$.

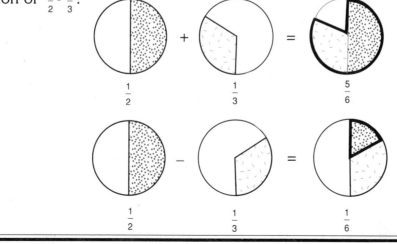

## Unit Bar Model

*Unit bars* have a standard length representing the whole. The bars are divided into fair shares (denominators) and the number under consideration (numerator) is shaded or colored. Addition consists of laying numerator sections end to end. Subtraction is done by finding the difference in length of the numerator sections.

The bars can be divided into any number of fair shares and therefore be used with any denominator.

The number line is an abstract form of the bar model.

## Unit Square Model

The *unit square model* is particularly useful for showing multiplication. It clarifies why the product of two proper fractions is less than either. This is troublesome to students until they see and understand what happens in the unit square model. The difference between the multiplication of whole numbers and the multiplication of proper fractions becomes clear.

The square has a measure of one unit along each side and an area of one square unit, representing the whole. The divisions along one side of the square indicate the denominator of one factor and the divisions along a perpendicular side the denominator of the second. Numerators for each are shaded in or colored. Their overlap is the numerator of the product and the total number of sections is the denominator as shown below where one-half is multiplied by two-thirds.

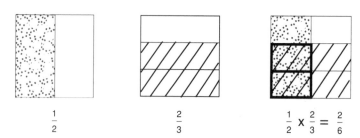

$$\frac{1}{2} \qquad \frac{2}{3} \qquad \frac{1}{2} \times \frac{2}{3} = \frac{2}{6}$$

## Set of Objects Model

The *set of objects model* mirrors many real-life situations such as determining what fractional part of the class is absent today or what fractional part of a class is girls. The total number in the set is the denominator and the number in the subset is the numerator.

## Egg Carton Model

Egg cartons come from the world with which students are familiar and bring with them important associations with that real world. The fact that egg cartons have twelve cavities makes them highly useful in the study of fractions, especially for their representation, addition, and subtraction. Halves, thirds, fourths, sixths, and twelfths are readily illustrated. These fractions and operations on them represent a majority of those students will meet in the real world.

## Geoboard and Coordinate Graph Model

This highly effective and interesting model is little known. It provides a greater array of connections among fractions, decimals, percents, ratios, and proportions than any other model. It is so rich as to require an extensive separate discussion in this publication.

Students will find that this model provides a synthesis of all of the important concepts associated with fractions, decimals, percents, ratios, proportions, tangents, slopes, etc.

## General Suggestions for Use

The central objective in all of the activities in this publication is to help students *build mental images of fractional parts and operations on fractions.* Such mental images serve them well when working at the abstract level, helping them to approximate answers and to avoid unreasonable ones.

Each of the models makes its unique contribution to the whole. Exposure to multiple models is important and is recommended in all of the reform documents. As students become familiar with the various models, they will find that some are more helpful in given situations than others. Together, they provide a powerful arsenal for achieving success in work with fractions.

The activities in this publication can be used in a variety of ways. Transparencies can be used effectively with the entire class to demonstrate processes and facilitate the development of mental imagery. For example, students can be shown a display of fractional parts, asked to estimate what part of the whole each represents, and what congruent shapes could be used to cover each. Such activities using any and all of the models are recommended as an effective way to help students build mental images.

The activity pages can be duplicated and laminated to become a permanent reusable resource. Individuals and small groups can draw from this inventory to work on those concepts, processes, and models to achieve mastery. The large number of activities provided for the development of specific concepts makes it possible to prescribe targeted practice to meet individual needs. Not every student needs to do all of the activities, only a sufficient number related to a given concept to acquire the desired level of proficiency.

The laminated activities can also be used for periodic review. Just as baseball players must return again and again to the practice of fundamentals so students must return again and again for practice on the fundamentals in work with fractions.

Where AIMS models are not available, card stock replicas can be made by duplicating the models included in the final section of this publication. Copies of the pattern block tiles can then be made using construction paper to match the color scheme used in the actual pattern blocks. If this scheme is used, students will be able to associate fractions both by color and by shape. It is advisable to also have a black set to remove the color cue in testing for shape only. The color scheme is: wholes – yellow; halves – red; thirds – blue; fourths – brown; sixths – green; twelfths – dark lavender.

*Part* **1**

# Modeling, Representing, Naming, and Ordering Non-Equivalent Fractions

In these activities students are introduced to five of the seven models they will be working with: hexagon, pie/circle, unit bar, unit square, and sets/subsets. Egg cartons and coordinate graph/geoboard models are reserved for treatment later.

It is recommended that activities be introduced to the entire class using overhead transparencies. Each aspect of the activity should be discussed thoroughly and fully understood before individual or small group work is begun. *Always keep in mind that the development of mental imagery is the primary objective!*

## Fraction Activities 1 – 6

Display the tiles (pattern blocks) on the overhead to help students learn to identify the respective fractional parts. Reference to the sides of the tiles is the key. The hexagon with six sides represents the whole. If the boundary includes three sides, the shape is a half. If it includes one and one-half sides, the shape is a fourth. Students can also be asked which shapes can be covered with congruent smaller shapes. This leads to the fundamental concept of equivalent fractions.

In these activities the white part of each hexagon is to be covered with the *fewest* possible congruent tiles. Students will discover that sometimes several sets of congruent tiles will cover the white part. If so, they have determined equivalent fractions. Under the given restriction, however, only the one solution is desired. Practice can be doubled by changing the instruction to cover the mottled portion instead of white portion.

Once the solution is determined, the modeled fraction is to be identified using symbolic notation. Finally, the relative magnitude of the two fractions is to be indicated. The ability to order fractions is another important skill.

Please duplicate the fraction tiles in the *Appendix* for use with the student activity pages.

## Fraction Activities 7 – 8

A slightly different approach is used in *Fraction Action 7* and *8* in that the fractional tile shape is represented. Students are to duplicate the representations with models, identify the fractions, and order sets of two fractions.

## Fraction Activities 9 – 19

In *Fraction Action 9 – 11*, students are to identify the complementary parts represented by unit bars, circles, and unit squares. This parallels the previous practice with hexagonal tiles. *Fraction Action 12* and *13* extend the identification of complementary parts to sets and subsets. In *14*, an inverse approach is used in which the indicated fractional part is to be shaded or colored. The three models, circles, bars, and unit squares, are interwoven to provide comparative practice. In activities *15 – 17*, models are constructed to represent the fractions named and all eight of the fractions are to be ordered. In *Fraction Action 18*, students are to build models of sets of two fractions using hexagon tiles, compare their magnitude, and express the relation between them. The first may be greater than, equal to, or less than the second. The same process is involved in activity *19* except that circle sectors are used as models.

# Fraction Action 1

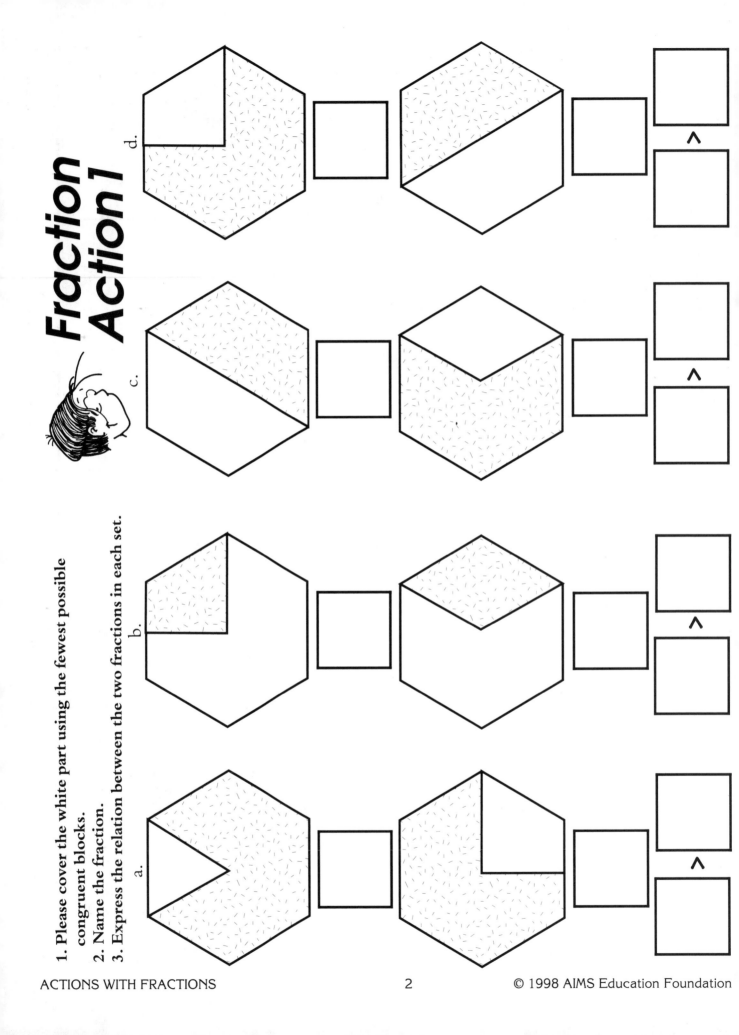

1. Please cover the white part using the fewest possible congruent blocks.
2. Name the fraction.
3. Express the relation between the two fractions in each set.

# Fraction Action 2

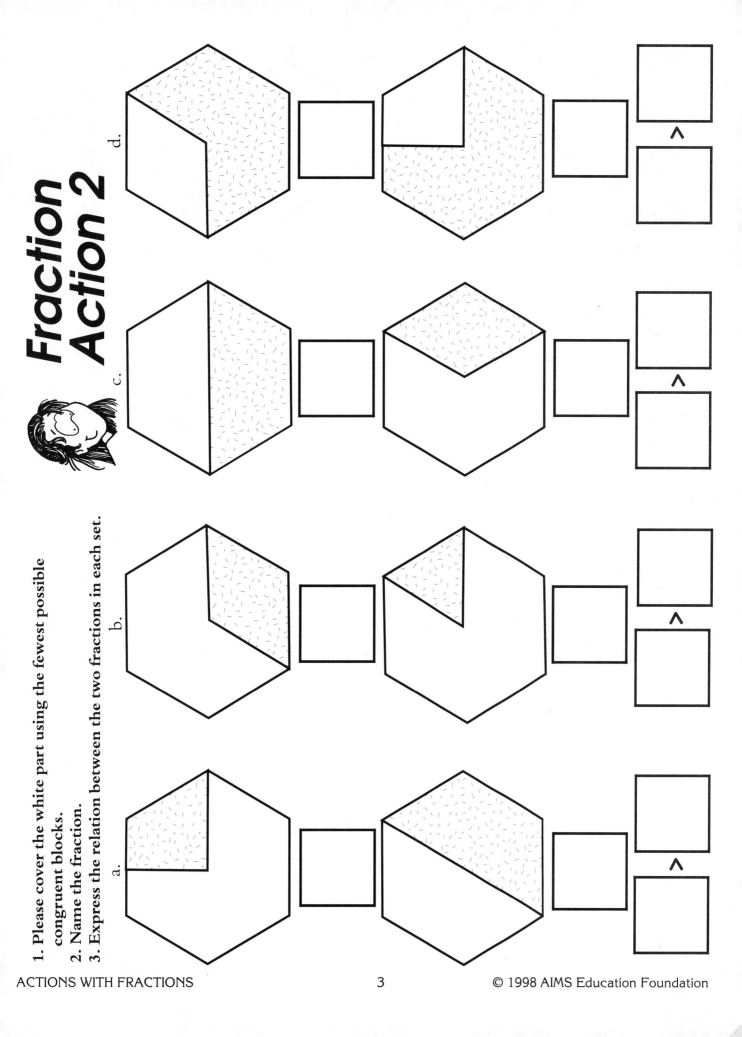

1. Please cover the white part using the fewest possible congruent blocks.
2. Name the fraction.
3. Express the relation between the two fractions in each set.

ACTIONS WITH FRACTIONS                    3                    © 1998 AIMS Education Foundation

# Fraction Action 3

1. Please cover the white part using the fewest possible congruent blocks.
2. Name the fraction.
3. Express the relation between the two fractions in each set.

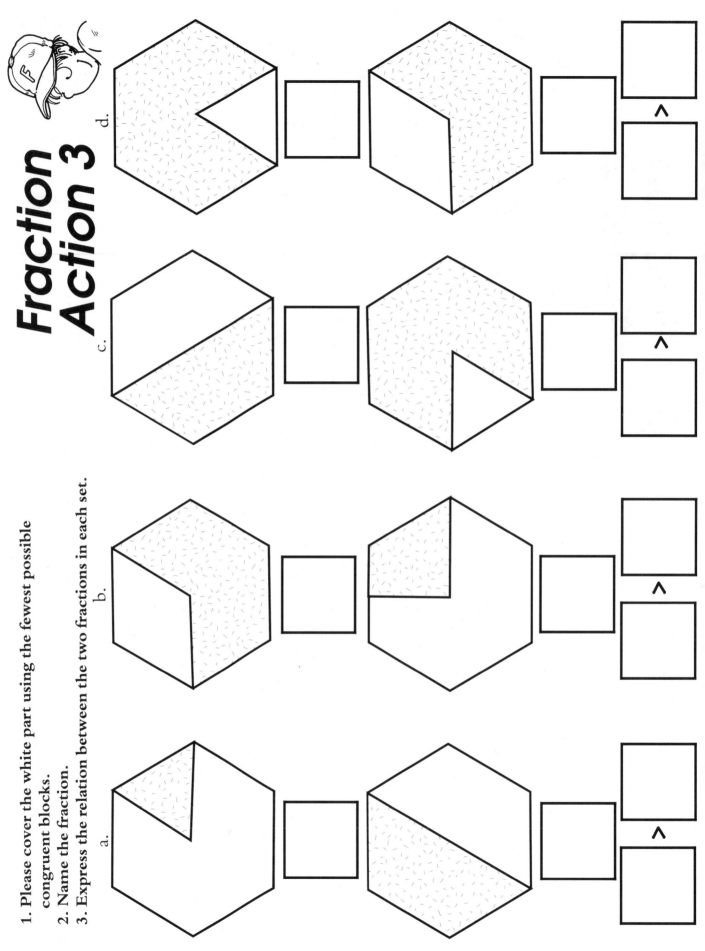

# Fraction Action 4

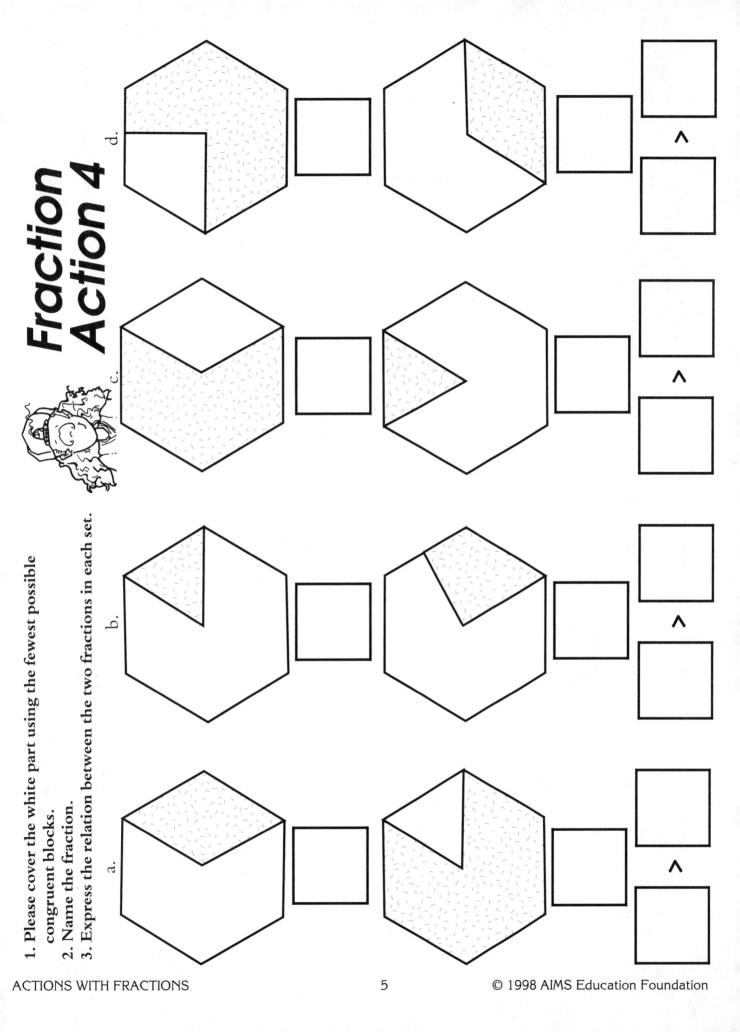

1. Please cover the white part using the fewest possible congruent blocks.
2. Name the fraction.
3. Express the relation between the two fractions in each set.

# Fraction Action 5

1. Please cover the white part using the fewest possible congruent blocks.
2. Name the fraction.
3. Express the relation between the two fractions in each set.

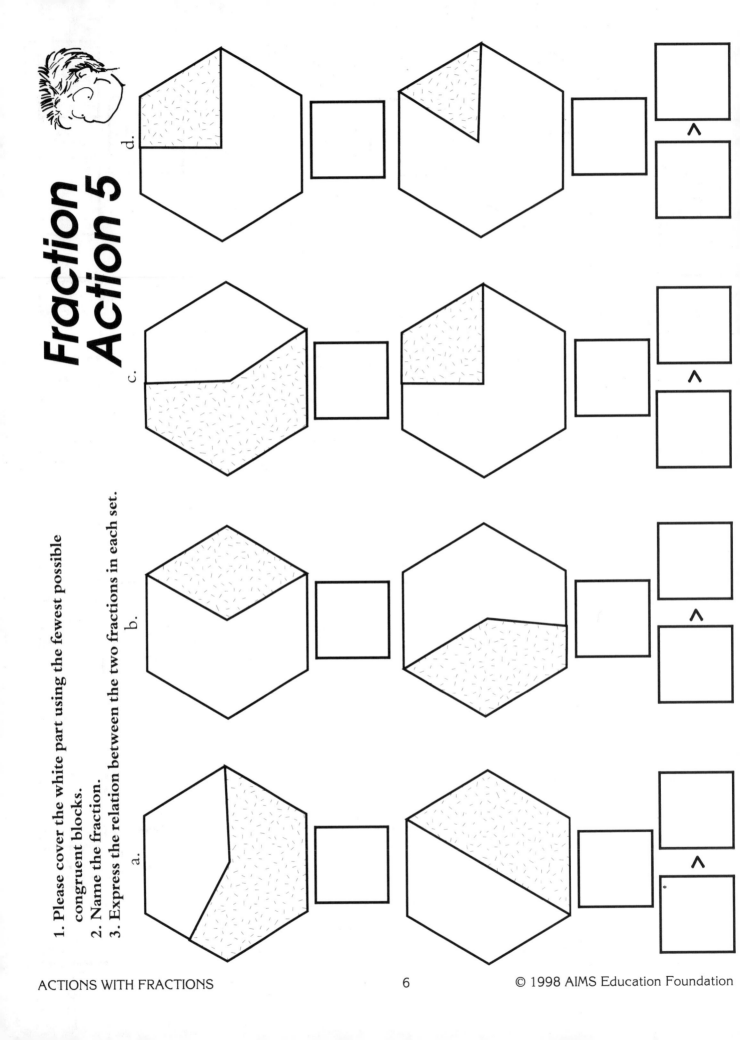

a.

☐   ☐ > ☐

b.

☐   ☐ > ☐

c.

☐   ☐ > ☐

d.

☐   ☐ > ☐

# Fraction Action 6

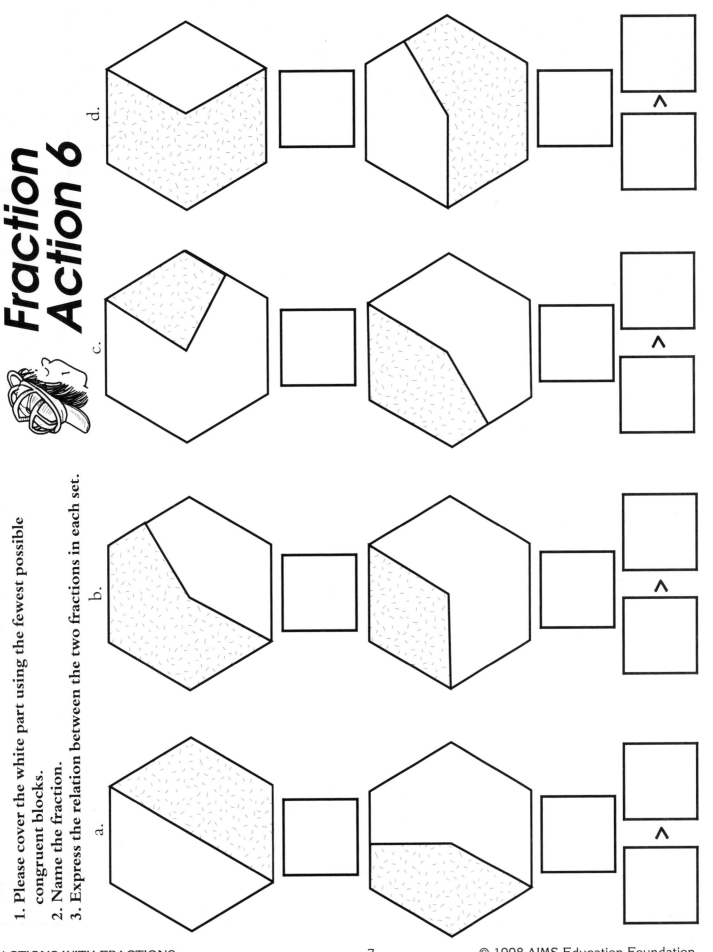

1. Please cover the white part using the fewest possible congruent blocks.
2. Name the fraction.
3. Express the relation between the two fractions in each set.

© 1998 AIMS Education Foundation

# Fraction
# Action 7

1. Please cover the white parts with blocks as shown.
2. Name the fraction.
3. Express the relation between the two fractions in each set.

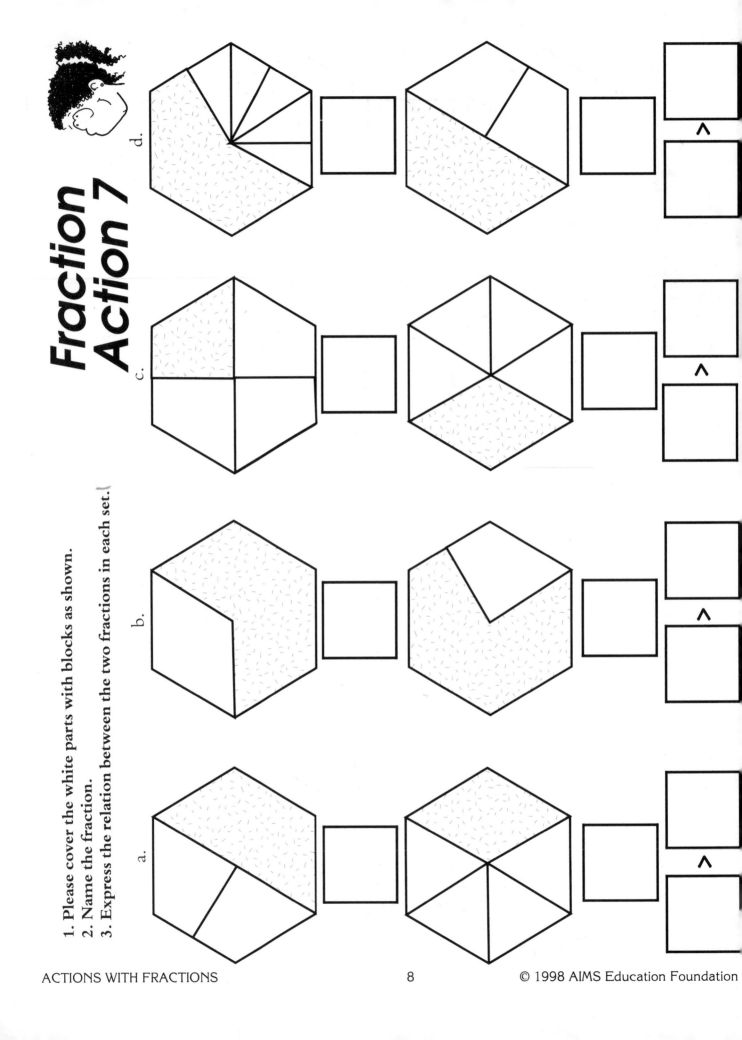

8

# Fraction
# Action 8

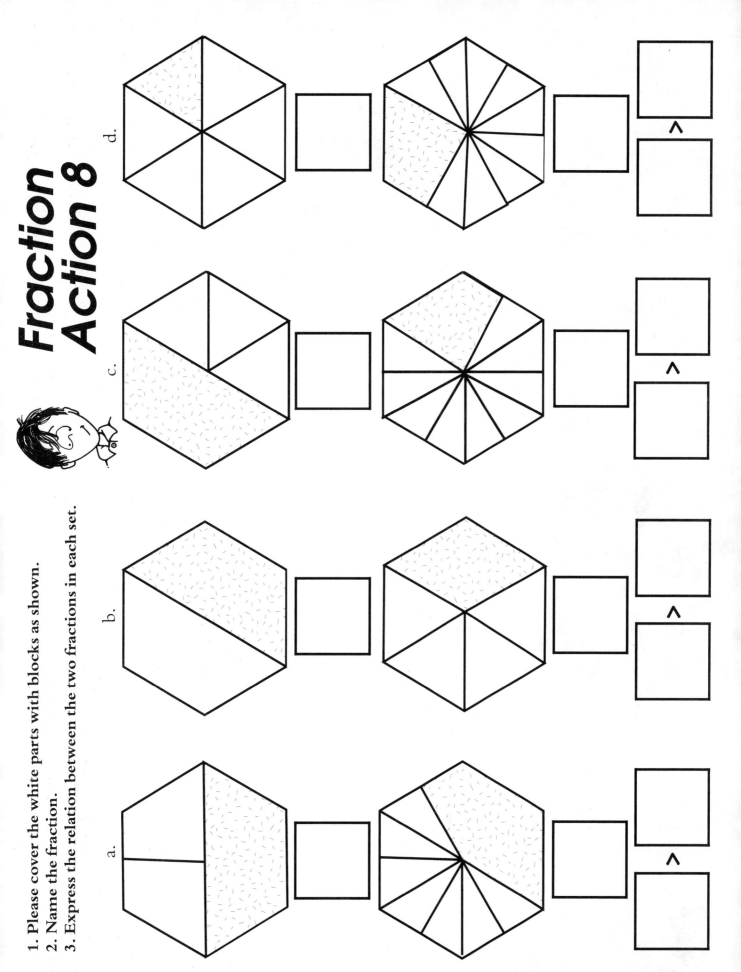

1. Please cover the white parts with blocks as shown.
2. Name the fraction.
3. Express the relation between the two fractions in each set.

# Fraction Action 9

Please write a fraction for
a. the unshaded part
b. the shaded part

1.
a. ——
b. ——

2.
a. ——
b. ——

3.
a. ——
b. ——

4.
a. ——
b. ——

5.
a. ——
b. ——

6.
a. ——
b. ——

7.
a. ——
b. ——

8.
a. ——
b. ——

9.
a. ——
b. ——

10.
a. ——
b. ——

11.
a. ——
b. ——

12.
a. ——
b. ——

13.
a. ——
b. ——

14.
a. ——
b. ——

15.
a. ——
b. ——

16.
a. ——
b. ——

$\dfrac{2}{3}$

ACTIONS WITH FRACTIONS

# Fraction Action 10

Please write a fraction for
a. the unshaded part
b. the shaded part

1.
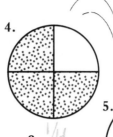
a. ½
b. ½

2.
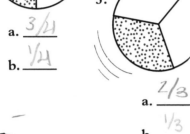
a. 3/4
b. ¼

3.
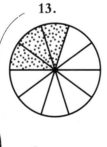
a. 2/3
b. ⅓

4.
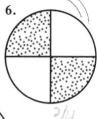
a. ¼
b. 3/4

5.

a. 5/6
b. ⅙

6.

a. 2/4
b. 2/4

7.
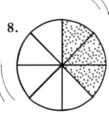
a. _____
b. _____

8.

a. _____
b. _____

9.
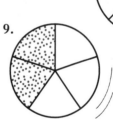
a. _____
b. _____

10.

a. _____
b. _____

11.
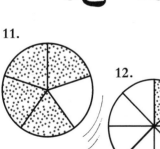
a. _____
b. _____

12.
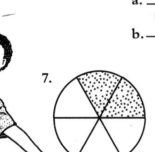
a. _____
b. _____

13.
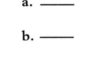
a. _____
b. _____

14.

a. _____
b. _____

15.
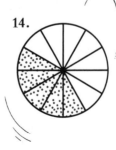
a. _____
b. _____

16.
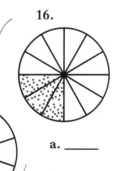
a. _____
b. _____

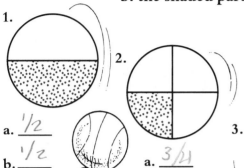

# Fraction
# Action 11

Please write a fraction for
 a. the unshaded part
 b. the shaded part

1.
a. ———
b. ———

2.
a. ———
b. ———

3.
a. ———
b. ———

4.
a. ———
b. ———

5.
a. ———
b. ———

6.
a. ———
b. ———

7.
a. ———
b. ———

8.
a. ———
b. ———

9.
a. ———
b. ———

10.
a. ———
b. ———

11.
a. ———
b. ———

12.
a. ———
b. ———

13.
a. ———
b. ———

14.
a. ———
b. ———

15.
a. ———
b. ———

16.
a. ———
b. ———

For each of the following sets, please
write a fraction representing the
subset of
   a. unshaded objects
   b. shaded objects

# Fraction Action 12

Example:

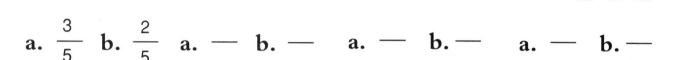

1. a. $\dfrac{3}{5}$   b. $\dfrac{2}{5}$    2. a. —   b. —    3. a. —   b. —    4. a. —   b. —

5. a. —   b. —    6. a. —   b. —    7. a. —   b. —    8. a. —   b. —

9. a. —   b. —    10. a. —   b. —    11. a. —   b. —    12. a. —   b. —

13. a. —   b. —    14. a. —   b. —    15. a. —   b. —    16. a. —   b. —

For each of the following sets, please write a fraction representing the subset of
   a. unshaded objects
   b. shaded objects

# Fraction Action 13

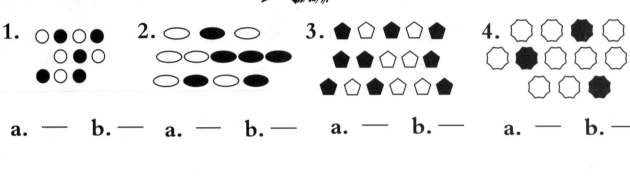

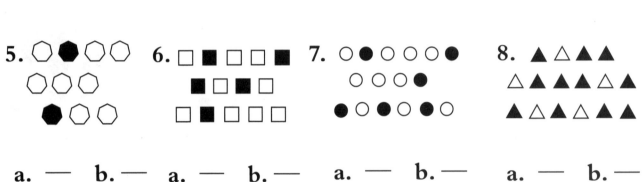

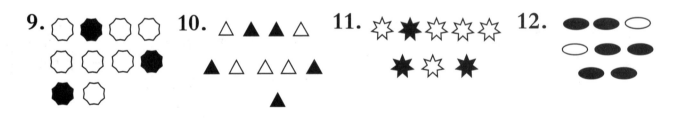

# Fraction Action 14

**Please shade in a picture of the fraction.**

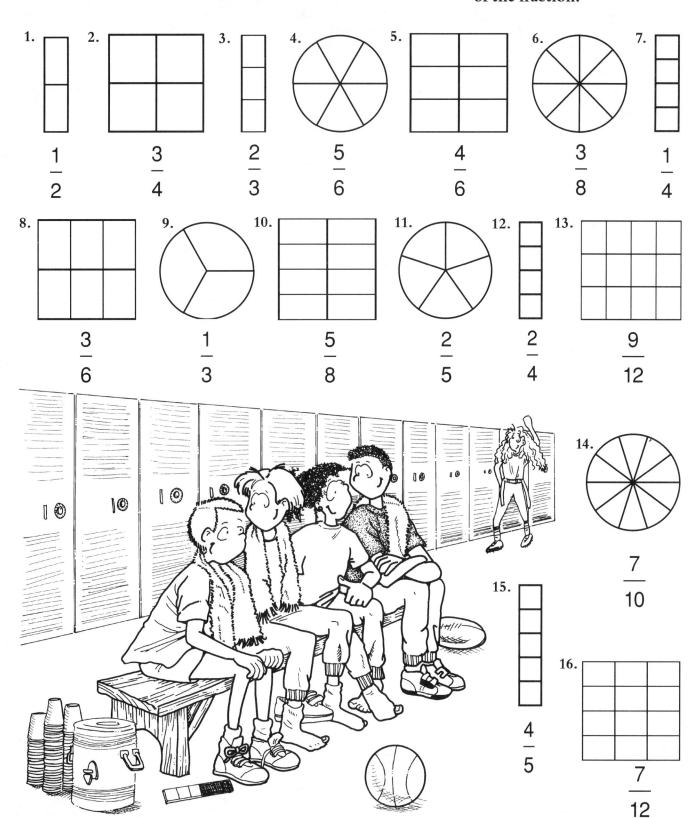

1. $\dfrac{1}{2}$

2. $\dfrac{3}{4}$

3. $\dfrac{2}{3}$

4. $\dfrac{5}{6}$

5. $\dfrac{4}{6}$

6. $\dfrac{3}{8}$

7. $\dfrac{1}{4}$

8. $\dfrac{3}{6}$

9. $\dfrac{1}{3}$

10. $\dfrac{5}{8}$

11. $\dfrac{2}{5}$

12. $\dfrac{2}{4}$

13. $\dfrac{9}{12}$

14. $\dfrac{7}{10}$

15. $\dfrac{4}{5}$

16. $\dfrac{7}{12}$

# Fraction Action 15

1. Please show the fractions named.
2. Arrange the eight fractions in order from greatest to least

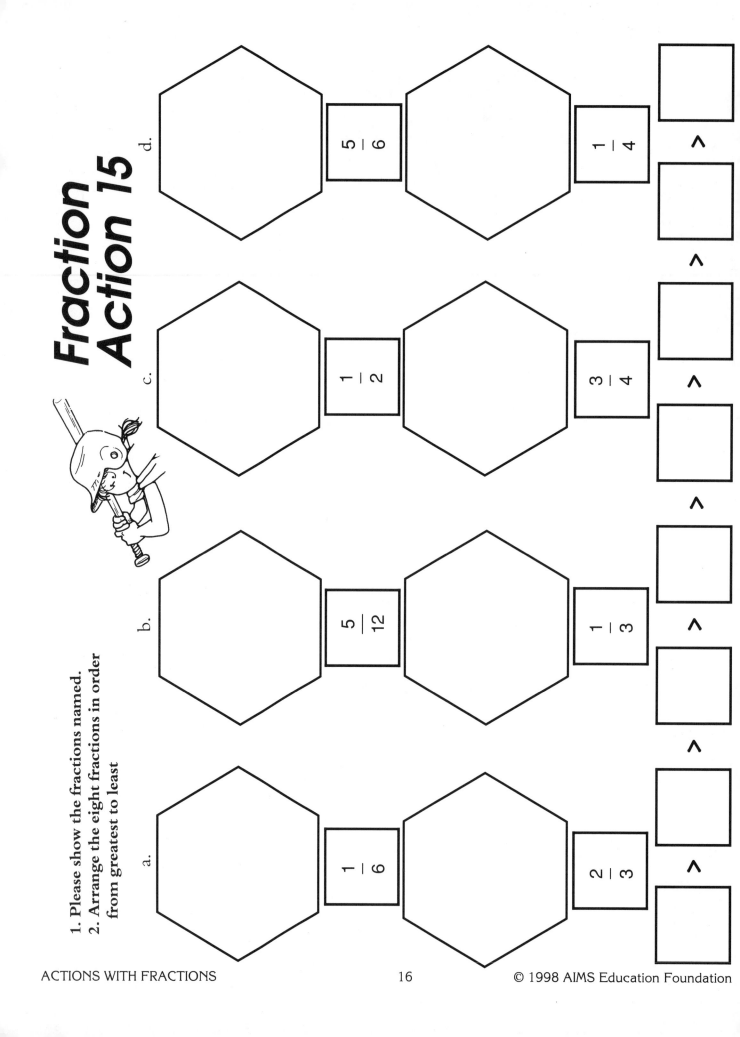

a.

$\dfrac{1}{6}$

$\dfrac{2}{3}$

b.

$\dfrac{5}{12}$

$\dfrac{1}{3}$

c.

$\dfrac{1}{2}$

$\dfrac{3}{4}$

d.

$\dfrac{5}{6}$

$\dfrac{1}{4}$

$> \quad > \quad > \quad > \quad > \quad > \quad >$

# Fraction Action 16

1. Please show the fractions named.
2. Arrange the eight fractions in order from greatest to least

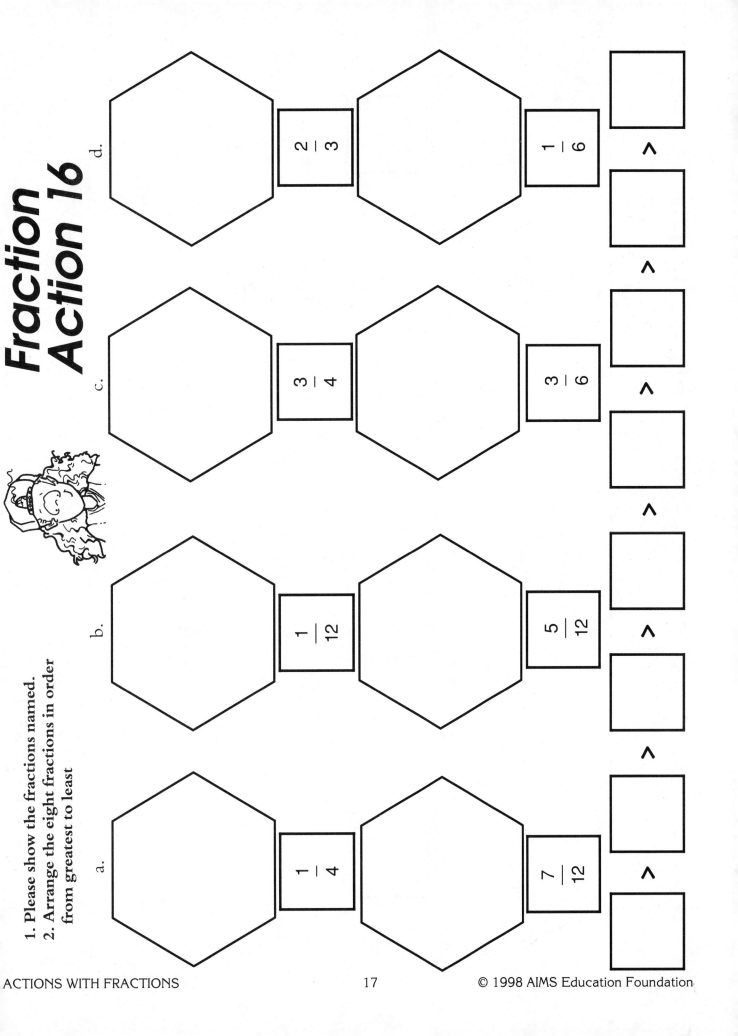

a.

$\dfrac{1}{4}$

$\dfrac{7}{12}$

b.

$\dfrac{1}{12}$

$\dfrac{5}{12}$

c.

$\dfrac{3}{4}$

$\dfrac{3}{6}$

d.

$\dfrac{2}{3}$

$\dfrac{1}{6}$

> > > > > > >

# Fraction Action 17

1. Please show the fractions named.
2. Arrange the eight fractions in order from greatest to least

a.

$\dfrac{5}{6}$

$\dfrac{7}{12}$

b.

$\dfrac{1}{12}$

$\dfrac{2}{6}$

c.

$\dfrac{11}{12}$

$\dfrac{9}{12}$

d.

$\dfrac{2}{3}$

$\dfrac{2}{4}$

___ > ___ > ___ > ___ > ___ > ___ > ___ > ___

# Fraction Action 18

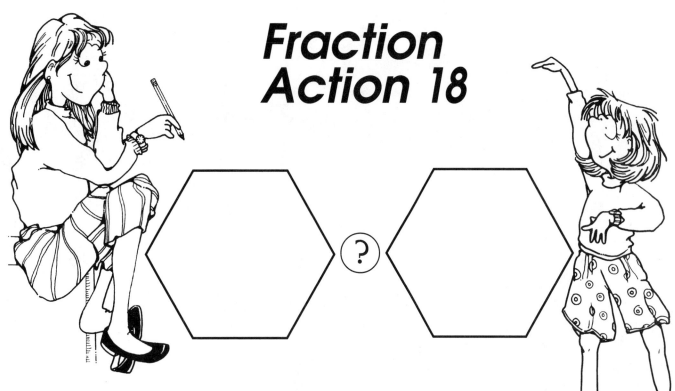

**Please compare the following, find the relation, and write
> , =, or < in the ◯ .**

1. $\dfrac{1}{2}$ ⟩ $\dfrac{1}{3}$

2. $\dfrac{1}{2}$ = $\dfrac{2}{4}$

3. $\dfrac{2}{4}$ ⟩ $\dfrac{1}{3}$

4. $\dfrac{2}{3}$ ⟩ $\dfrac{3}{6}$

5. $\dfrac{5}{6}$ ◯ $\dfrac{2}{3}$

6. $\dfrac{3}{4}$ ◯ $\dfrac{1}{2}$

7. $\dfrac{2}{6}$ ◯ $\dfrac{1}{2}$

8. $\dfrac{1}{4}$ ◯ $\dfrac{1}{6}$

9. $\dfrac{4}{6}$ ◯ $\dfrac{1}{2}$

10. $\dfrac{2}{3}$ ◯ $\dfrac{2}{4}$

11. $\dfrac{4}{6}$ ◯ $\dfrac{2}{3}$

12. $\dfrac{3}{4}$ ◯ $\dfrac{2}{3}$

13. $\dfrac{1}{3}$ ◯ $\dfrac{1}{6}$

14. $\dfrac{1}{2}$ ◯ $\dfrac{3}{6}$

15. $\dfrac{1}{3}$ ◯ $\dfrac{1}{4}$

16. $\dfrac{1}{2}$ ◯ $\dfrac{1}{4}$

# Fraction Action 19

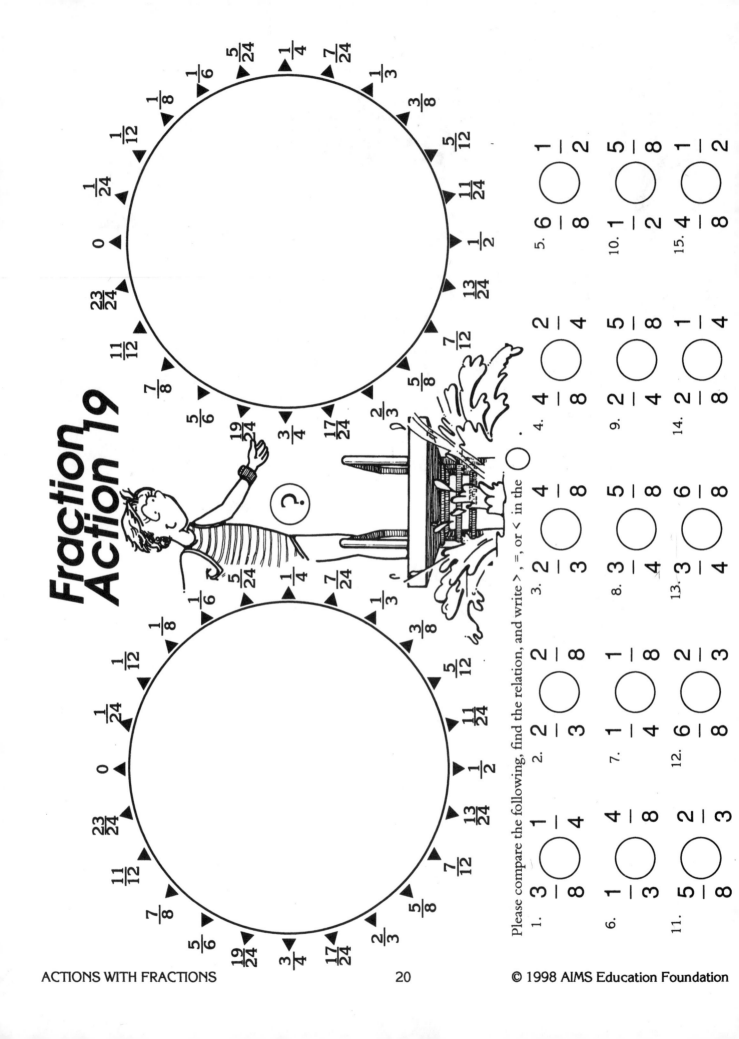

Please compare the following, find the relation, and write >, =, or < in the ○ .

1. $\dfrac{3}{8}$ ○ $\dfrac{1}{4}$

2. $\dfrac{2}{3}$ ○ $\dfrac{2}{8}$

3. $\dfrac{2}{3}$ ○ $\dfrac{4}{8}$

4. $\dfrac{4}{8}$ ○ $\dfrac{2}{4}$

5. $\dfrac{6}{8}$ ○ $\dfrac{1}{2}$

6. $\dfrac{1}{3}$ ○ $\dfrac{4}{8}$

7. $\dfrac{1}{4}$ ○ $\dfrac{1}{8}$

8. $\dfrac{3}{4}$ ○ $\dfrac{5}{8}$

9. $\dfrac{2}{4}$ ○ $\dfrac{5}{8}$

10. $\dfrac{1}{2}$ ○ $\dfrac{5}{8}$

11. $\dfrac{5}{8}$ ○ $\dfrac{2}{3}$

12. $\dfrac{6}{8}$ ○ $\dfrac{2}{3}$

13. $\dfrac{3}{4}$ ○ $\dfrac{6}{8}$

14. $\dfrac{2}{8}$ ○ $\dfrac{1}{4}$

15. $\dfrac{4}{8}$ ○ $\dfrac{1}{2}$

# Part 2

## Modeling, Representing, and Naming Equivalent Fractions

In this section, the focus shifts to the identification of equivalent fractions. Equivalent fractions and ratios play such a basic role in mathematics that it is of fundamental importance for students to acquire facility in their identification. Renaming to make addition and subtraction possible and forming proportions are only two of numerous applications where this skill is required.

In *Fraction Action 20* and *21*, equivalent white spaces are to be covered with two different sets of congruent tiles and each fraction modeled is to be identified. (Practice can be extended by covering the mottled portion instead.) In activities *22 – 24*, one fraction is named and it together with an equivalent fraction are to be modeled and named. *Fraction Action 25* is entirely open-ended, permitting the student to model and identify any fraction and an equivalent fraction.

In *Fraction Action 26*, the first unit bar is divided into shaded and unshaded parts. Students are to shade the second bar to match the first. The two shaded and unshaded sets of equivalents fractions are to be identified. The same process is used with circles in *Fraction Action 27*. Unit square representations are used in activity *28* to show up to five equivalent fractions in each case. In activity *29*, the inverse approach is used in that equivalent fractions are named. Students are to color or shade in representations of each and compare the pictures for relative size.

With the foregoing experiences that relate the manipulative, representational, and abstract expressions of fractions, students are prepared to move to the abstract reasoning called for in *Fraction Action 30* and *31. The emphasis should be on proportional reasoning rather than the cross-multiplication algorithm.* The algorithm is to be used only for checking. To encourage proportional reasoning, it must be modeled. This can be done by using the following approach. Given the problem:

$$\frac{5}{6} = \frac{\phantom{24}}{24}$$

think, "Six is multiplied by 4 to get 24, so 5 must be multiplied by 4 to determine the second numerator. The result is that $\frac{20}{24}$ is equivalent to $\frac{5}{6}$." Repetition of this type of reasoning helps to build toward the use of proportional reasoning in subsequent applications. Again, cross-multiplication should be used only after this type of proportional reasoning has been employed.

# Fraction
# Action 20

1. Please cover the white space in the left hexagon with congruent blocks.
2. Cover the white space in the right hexagon with congruent blocks of another kind.
3. Name the fraction.

a.

b.

c.

d.

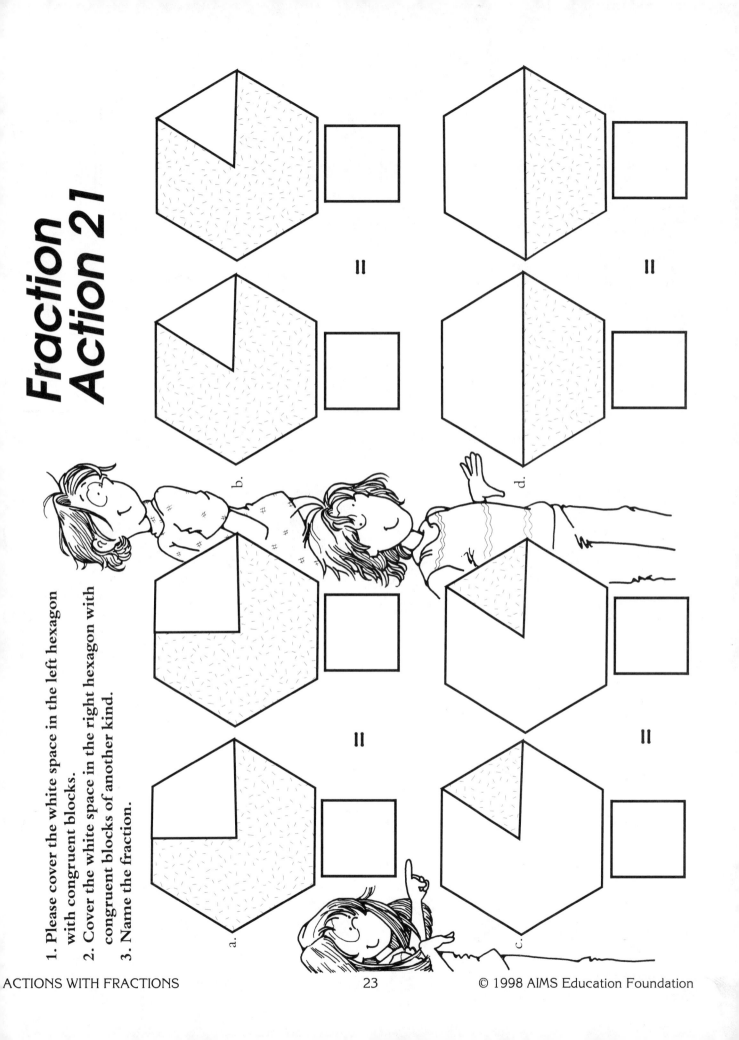

# Fraction
# Action 21

1. Please cover the white space in the left hexagon with congruent blocks.
2. Cover the white space in the right hexagon with congruent blocks of another kind.
3. Name the fraction.

a.

b.

c.

d.

23

# Fraction
# Action 22

1. Please show the named fraction.
2. In the right hexagon, please build an equivalent fraction.
3. Name the second fraction.

a.  ⬡  =  ⬡
    $\frac{1}{2}$  ☐

b.  ⬡  =  ⬡
    $\frac{1}{3}$  ☐

c.  ⬡  =  ⬡
    $\frac{2}{3}$  ☐

d.  ⬡  =  ⬡
    $\frac{1}{6}$  ☐

24

# Fraction Action 23

1. Please show the named fraction.
2. In the right hexagon, please build an equivalent fraction.
3. Name the second fraction.

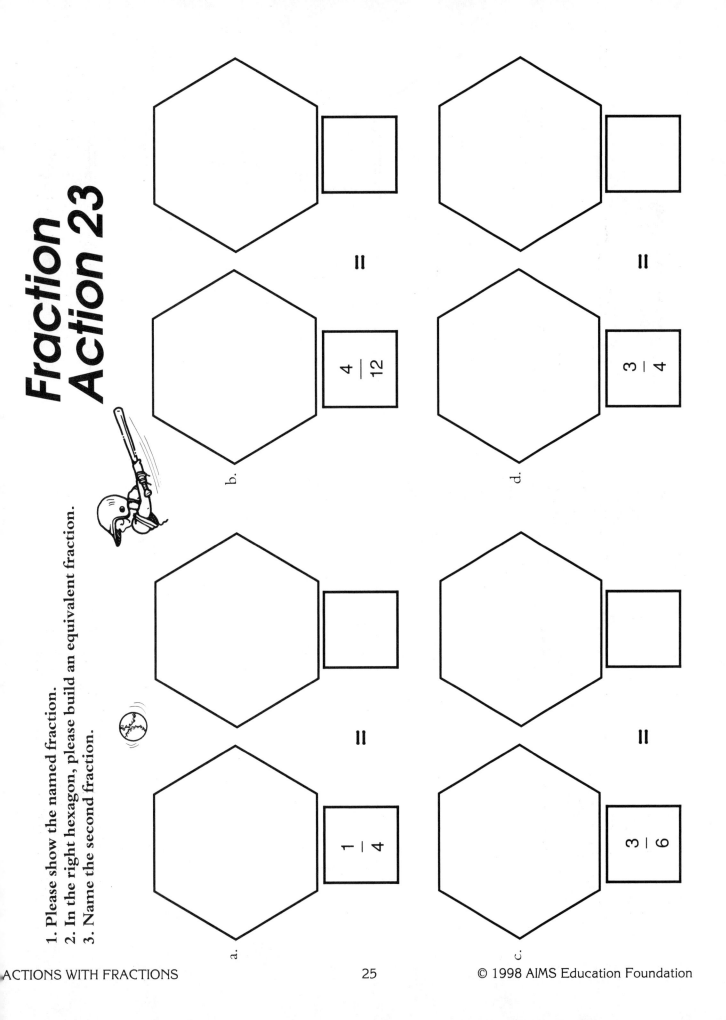

a.  ⬡ = ⬡  $\dfrac{1}{4}$

b.  ⬡ = ⬡  $\dfrac{4}{12}$

c.  ⬡ = ⬡  $\dfrac{3}{6}$

d.  ⬡ = ⬡  $\dfrac{3}{4}$

# Fraction
# Action 24

1. Please show the named fraction.
2. In the right hexagon, please build an equivalent fraction.
3. Name the second fraction.

a.

$$\frac{10}{12}$$

=

b.

$$\frac{9}{12}$$

=

c.

$$\frac{6}{12}$$

=

d.

$$\frac{8}{12}$$

=

26

# Fraction Action 25

1. Please cover a part of the left hexagon with congruent blocks.
2. Cover a congruent part of the right hexagon with congruent blocks of another kind.
3. Name the fractions.

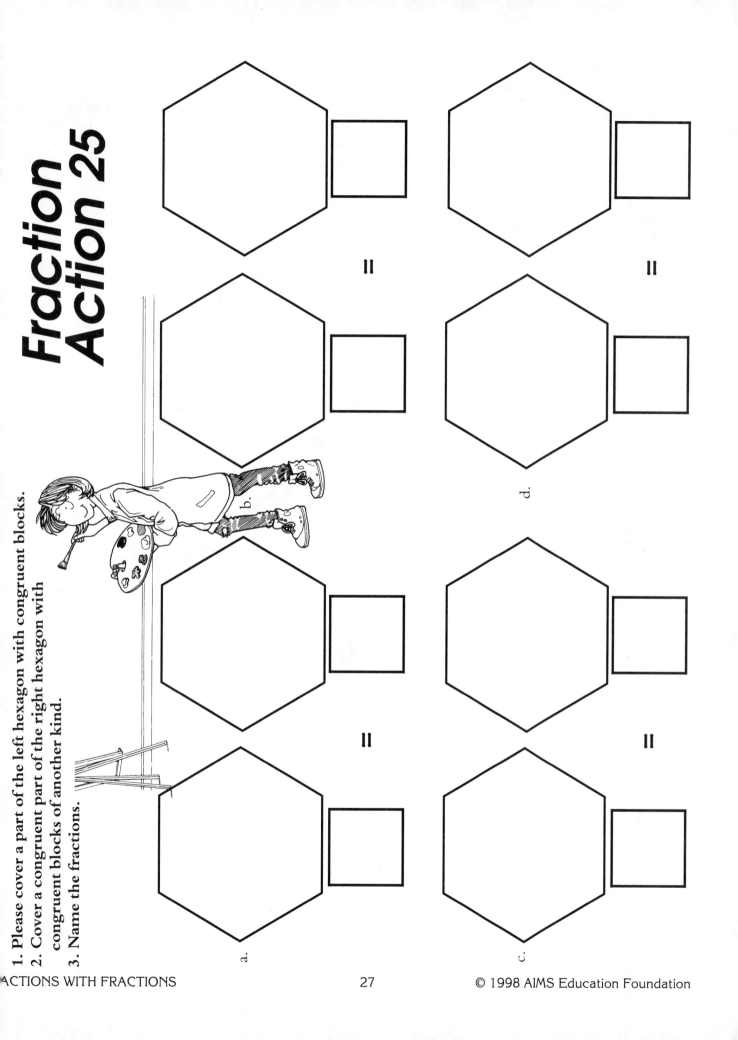

a.  =

b.  =

c.  =

d.  =

# Fraction Action 26

Please shade a region in the second bar to match the first. Then write a sentence describing the equivalent fractions for:  a. the unshaded part;  b. the shaded part.

Example:

 1. 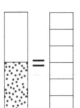 2.  3. 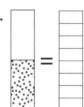 4. 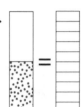 5.  6.

a. $\dfrac{1}{2} = \dfrac{2}{4}$    a. $\underline{\phantom{0}} = \underline{\phantom{0}}$    a. $\underline{\phantom{0}} = \underline{\phantom{0}}$    a. $\underline{\phantom{0}} = \underline{\phantom{0}}$    a. $\underline{\phantom{0}} = \underline{\phantom{0}}$    a. $\underline{\phantom{0}} = \underline{\phantom{0}}$

b. $\dfrac{1}{2} = \dfrac{2}{4}$    b. $\underline{\phantom{0}} = \underline{\phantom{0}}$    b. $\underline{\phantom{0}} = \underline{\phantom{0}}$    b. $\underline{\phantom{0}} = \underline{\phantom{0}}$    b. $\underline{\phantom{0}} = \underline{\phantom{0}}$    b. $\underline{\phantom{0}} = \underline{\phantom{0}}$

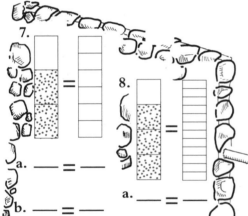

7.

a. $\underline{\phantom{0}} = \underline{\phantom{0}}$

b. $\underline{\phantom{0}} = \underline{\phantom{0}}$

8.

a. $\underline{\phantom{0}} = \underline{\phantom{0}}$

b. $\underline{\phantom{0}} = \underline{\phantom{0}}$

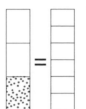 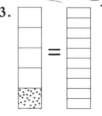  

9.

a. $\underline{\phantom{0}} = \underline{\phantom{0}}$

b. $\underline{\phantom{0}} = \underline{\phantom{0}}$

10.

a. $\underline{\phantom{0}} = \underline{\phantom{0}}$

b. $\underline{\phantom{0}} = \underline{\phantom{0}}$

11.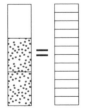

a. $\underline{\phantom{0}} = \underline{\phantom{0}}$

b. $\underline{\phantom{0}} = \underline{\phantom{0}}$

12.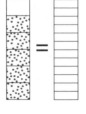

a. $\underline{\phantom{0}} = \underline{\phantom{0}}$

b. $\underline{\phantom{0}} = \underline{\phantom{0}}$

13.

a. $\underline{\phantom{0}} = \underline{\phantom{0}}$

b. $\underline{\phantom{0}} = \underline{\phantom{0}}$

14.

a. $\underline{\phantom{0}} = \underline{\phantom{0}}$

b. $\underline{\phantom{0}} = \underline{\phantom{0}}$

# Fraction Action 27

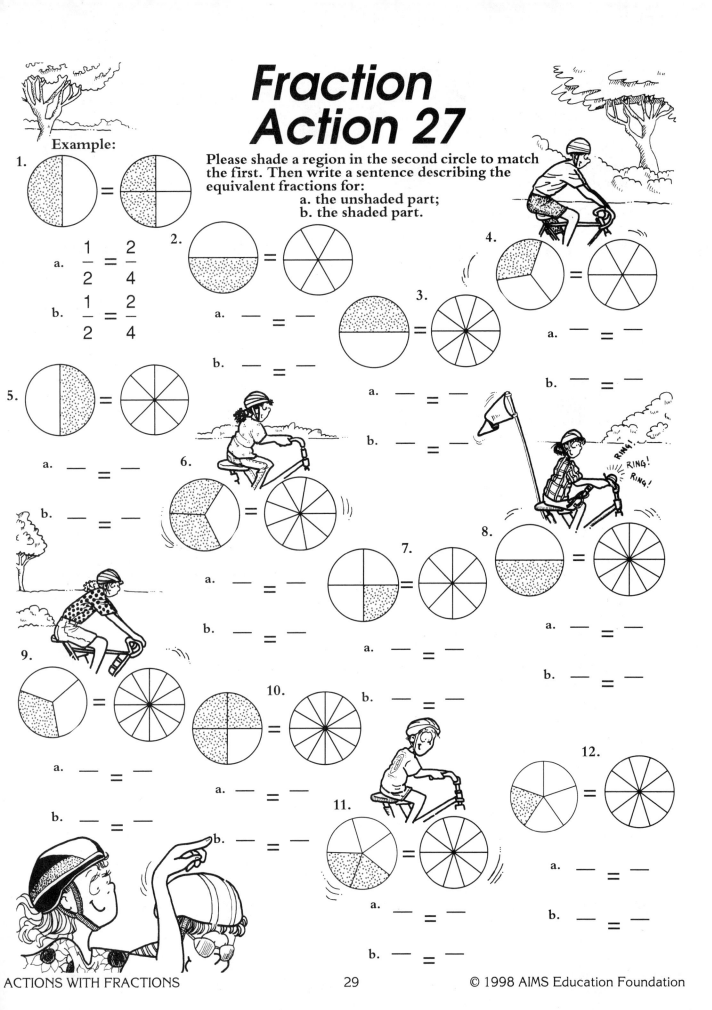

**Example:**

1. $\bigodot = \bigodot$

Please shade a region in the second circle to match the first. Then write a sentence describing the equivalent fractions for:
  a. the unshaded part;
  b. the shaded part.

a. $\dfrac{1}{2} = \dfrac{2}{4}$

b. $\dfrac{1}{2} = \dfrac{2}{4}$

2. $\bigcirc = \bigcirc$
  a. ___ = ___
  b. ___ = ___

3. $\bigcirc = \bigcirc$
  a. ___ = ___
  b. ___ = ___

4. $\bigcirc = \bigcirc$
  a. ___ = ___
  b. ___ = ___

5. $\bigcirc = \bigcirc$
  a. ___ = ___
  b. ___ = ___

6. $\bigcirc = \bigcirc$
  a. ___ = ___
  b. ___ = ___

7. $\bigcirc = \bigcirc$
  a. ___ = ___
  b. ___ = ___

8. $\bigcirc = \bigcirc$
  a. ___ = ___
  b. ___ = ___

9. $\bigcirc = \bigcirc$
  a. ___ = ___
  b. ___ = ___

10. $\bigcirc = \bigcirc$
  a. ___ = ___
  b. ___ = ___

11. $\bigcirc = \bigcirc$
  a. ___ = ___
  b. ___ = ___

12. $\bigcirc = \bigcirc$
  a. ___ = ___
  b. ___ = ___

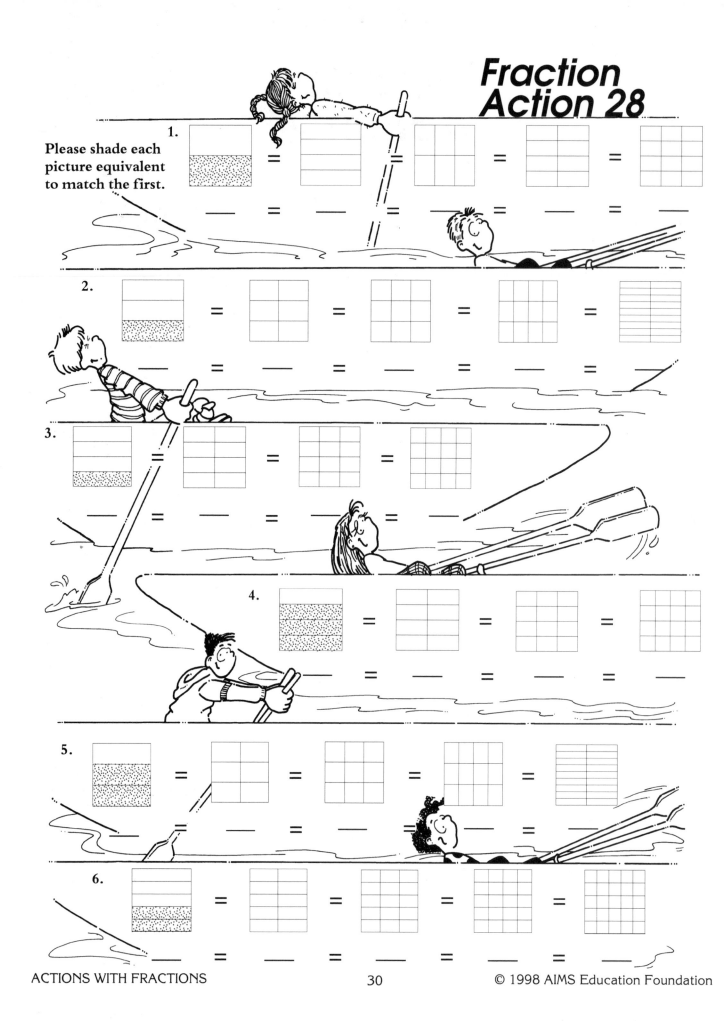

# Fraction Action 28

1. Please shade each picture equivalent to match the first.

ACTIONS WITH FRACTIONS

30

© 1998 AIMS Education Foundation

# Fraction
# Action 29

Please color the indicated fraction of
each circle. Compare the results.

How do they
compare?

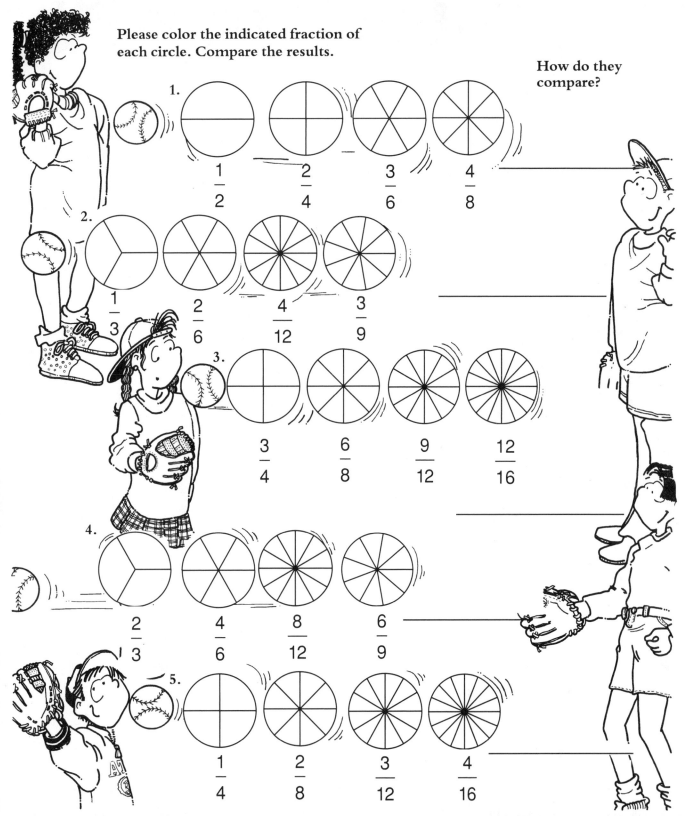

1.

$\frac{1}{2}$   $\frac{2}{4}$   $\frac{3}{6}$   $\frac{4}{8}$

2.

$\frac{1}{3}$   $\frac{2}{6}$   $\frac{4}{12}$   $\frac{3}{9}$

3.

$\frac{3}{4}$   $\frac{6}{8}$   $\frac{9}{12}$   $\frac{12}{16}$

4.

$\frac{2}{3}$   $\frac{4}{6}$   $\frac{8}{12}$   $\frac{6}{9}$

5.

$\frac{1}{4}$   $\frac{2}{8}$   $\frac{3}{12}$   $\frac{4}{16}$

Please find the missing terms that are
necessary to form equivalent fractions.
Check your answer by finding the cross-products.

# Fraction
# Action 30

Example:

$$\frac{1}{2} = \frac{}{6}$$

$$\frac{1}{2} = \frac{3}{6}$$

$$2 \times 3 = 1 \times 6$$

$$6 = 6$$

1.  $\dfrac{2}{3} = \dfrac{}{9}$

— x — = — x —

— = —

2.  $\dfrac{3}{4} = \dfrac{}{12}$

— x — = — x —

— = —

3.  $\dfrac{1}{3} = \dfrac{}{12}$

— x — = — x —

— = —

4.  $\dfrac{1}{2} = \dfrac{}{8}$

— x — = — x —

— = —

5.  $\dfrac{1}{4} = \dfrac{}{8}$

— x — = — x —

— = —

6.  $\dfrac{3}{4} = \dfrac{}{16}$

— x — = — x —

— = —

7.  $\dfrac{2}{5} = \dfrac{}{15}$

— x — = — x —

— = —

8.  $\dfrac{2}{3} = \dfrac{}{24}$

— x — = — x —

— = —

9.  $\dfrac{1}{6} = \dfrac{}{12}$

— x — = — x —

— = —

10. $\dfrac{1}{2} = \dfrac{}{12}$

— x — = — x —

— = —

11. $\dfrac{1}{4} = \dfrac{}{24}$

— x — = — x —

— = —

12. $\dfrac{3}{5} = \dfrac{}{20}$

— x — = — x —

— = —

13. $\dfrac{5}{6} = \dfrac{}{12}$

— x — = — x —

— = —

14. $\dfrac{3}{8} = \dfrac{}{16}$

— x — = — x —

— = —

Please find the missing terms that are necessary to form equivalent fractions. Check your answer by finding the cross-products.

# Fraction Action 31

1. $\dfrac{5}{6} = \dfrac{\ }{24}$

___ x ___ = ___ x ___

___ = ___

2. $\dfrac{\ }{8} = \dfrac{21}{24}$

___ x ___ = ___ x ___

___ = ___

3. $\dfrac{5}{\ } = \dfrac{15}{24}$

___ x ___ = ___ x ___

___ = ___

4. $\dfrac{1}{2} = \dfrac{5}{10}$

___ x ___ = ___ x ___

___ = ___

5. $\dfrac{2}{3} = \dfrac{8}{\ }$

___ x ___ = ___ x ___

___ = ___

6. $\dfrac{\ }{6} = \dfrac{16}{24}$

___ x ___ = ___ x ___

___ = ___

7. $\dfrac{4}{\ } = \dfrac{16}{20}$

___ x ___ = ___ x ___

___ = ___

8. $\dfrac{3}{4} = \dfrac{6}{\ }$

___ x ___ = ___ x ___

___ = ___

9. $\dfrac{15}{18} = \dfrac{\ }{6}$

___ x ___ = ___ x ___

___ = ___

10. $\dfrac{21}{24} = \dfrac{\ }{8}$

___ x ___ = ___ x ___

___ = ___

11. $\dfrac{6}{16} = \dfrac{\ }{8}$

___ x ___ = ___ x ___

___ = ___

12. $\dfrac{8}{24} = \dfrac{\ }{3}$

___ x ___ = ___ x ___

___ = ___

13. $\dfrac{10}{25} = \dfrac{\ }{5}$

___ x ___ = ___ x ___

___ = ___

14. $\dfrac{\ }{3} = \dfrac{10}{15}$

___ x ___ = ___ x ___

___ = ___

15. $\dfrac{21}{28} = \dfrac{\ }{4}$

___ x ___ = ___ x ___

___ = ___

# Part 3

## Part + Part = Whole
## Addition of Fractions

Addition here uses the part + part = whole approach. This is evidenced in the manipulative activities where the two parts are first modeled and then added by joining the parts in a third space. The meaning of "+" is modeled by the movement joining the parts.

In *Fraction Action 32 – 35*, the white parts are to be covered with the fewest possible congruent tiles and the fractions named. Next, the parts are joined by moving them into the "whole" hexagon. If the tiles in the parts are different, they must exchanged for the *fewest* congruent tiles in representing the sum. This is the manipulative counterpart of renaming a fraction to lowest terms. Where the sum is greater than one, the first coupled hexagon is filled and any remaining tiles are placed into the second. The result is a mixed fraction.

The inverse approach is used in activities *36 – 39*. The named fractional parts are to be modeled using the fewest congruent tiles for each. Then the parts are joined as before and the sentence is completed.

Pie slices and a fraction clock are the manipulatives used in *Fraction Action 40 – 46*. Laying end to end is the process. The suggested procedure is to first use mental images to find the sum. This can be reinforced by using pie slices to check the answer. For this, the pie slice corresponding to each addend is selected. In any order, a first slice is placed into the clock beginning at zero and extending clockwise. The second is joined (placed end to end) to the far end of the first and continues the clockwise covering. The end point of the second is the sum and is read off the clock. Finally, the sum is recorded.

In *Fraction Action 47* and *48*, the process is completed at the representation level without the use of manipulatives. The sum is colored or shaded and the parts and sum are named in the sentence. In activity *49*, the parts are first represented by coloring in using distinguishing colors and the sum is named. The number of sections in the circle parallels the lowest common denominator. In the coloring process an equivalent fraction frequently becomes apparent.

*Fraction Action 50* is an open-ended activity in which students select the fractional parts either by the notation or representation and then complete the representational and abstract description.

In *Fraction Action 51* and *52*, addition is modeled using fraction rulers. First, the students are asked to solve the problems using the standard algorithm. Then the answers are checked using the rulers. (Additional rulers are found in the *Appendix*.)

With fraction rulers, addition consists of laying numerator parts end to end. The endpoint of the first addend is located on the affixed ruler. The zero point of the moveable ruler (found in the *Appendix*) is placed at this endpoint with the ruler extending upward. The endpoint of the second addend is located on the moveable ruler and the sum is read on the affixed ruler opposite this point.

*Fraction Action 53* is another activity in which a partial statement that includes the two addends is to be matched with its representation in unit square form. The sum is first determined at the abstract level and then checked against its representational counterpart.

# Fraction Action 32

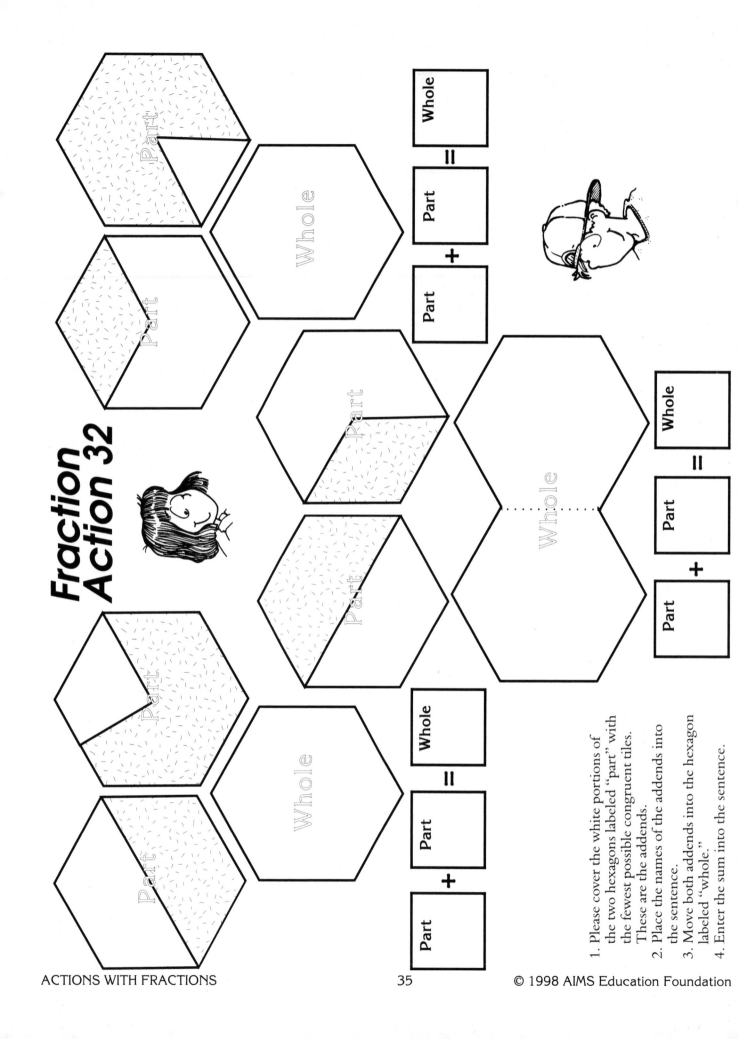

Part + Part = Whole

Part + Part = Whole

Part + Part = Whole

1. Please cover the white portions of the two hexagons labeled "part" with the fewest possible congruent tiles. These are the addends.

2. Place the names of the addends into the sentence.

3. Move both addends into the hexagon labeled "whole."

4. Enter the sum into the sentence.

# Fraction Action 33

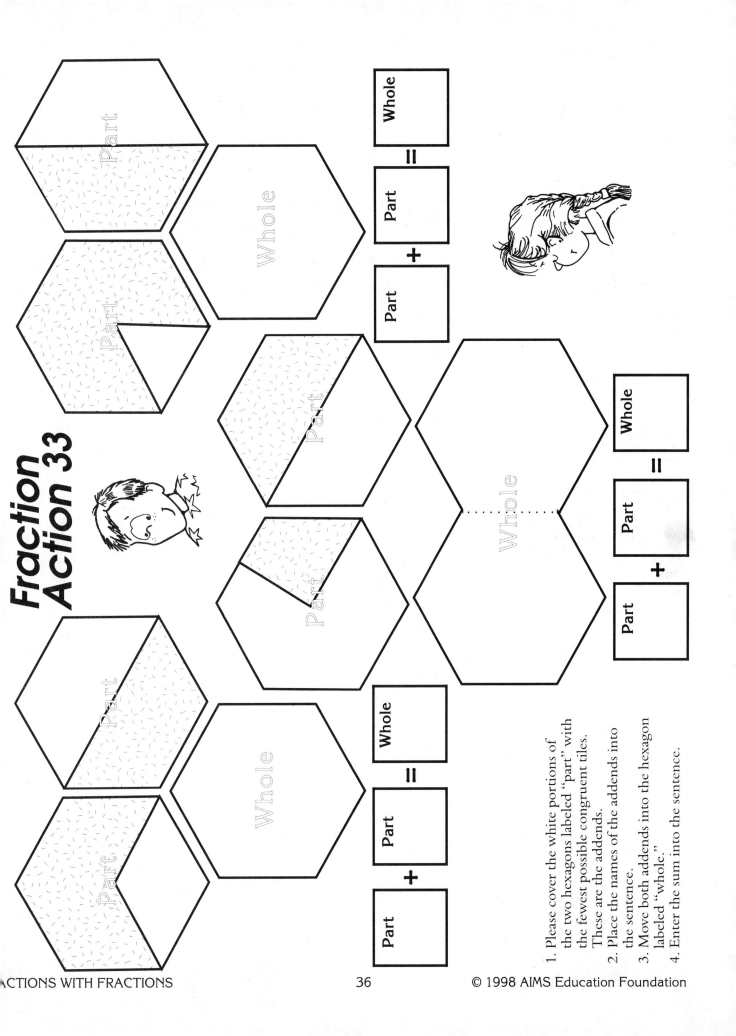

Part

Part

Whole

Part + Part = Whole

Part

Part

Whole

Part + Part = Whole

Whole

Part

Part

Part + Part = Whole

1. Please cover the white portions of the two hexagons labeled "part" with the fewest possible congruent tiles. These are the addends.
2. Place the names of the addends into the sentence.
3. Move both addends into the hexagon labeled "whole."
4. Enter the sum into the sentence.

# Fraction Action 34

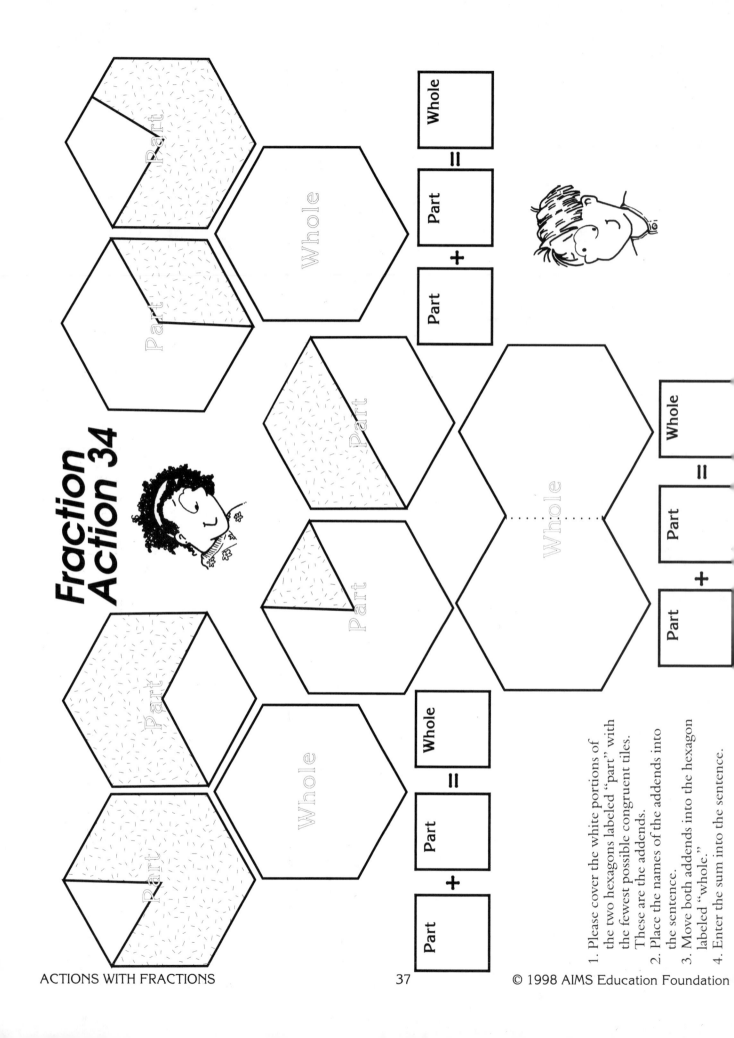

Part

Part

Whole

| Part | + | Part | = | Whole |
|------|---|------|---|-------|

Part

Part

Whole

Part

Part

Whole

| Part | + | Part | = | Whole |
|------|---|------|---|-------|

| Part | + | Part | = | Whole |
|------|---|------|---|-------|

1. Please cover the white portions of the two hexagons labeled "part" with the fewest possible congruent tiles. These are the addends.
2. Place the names of the addends into the sentence.
3. Move both addends into the hexagon labeled "whole."
4. Enter the sum into the sentence.

ACTIONS WITH FRACTIONS

37

© 1998 AIMS Education Foundation

# Fraction Action 35

| Part | + | Part | = | Whole |
|------|---|------|---|-------|
|      |   |      |   |       |

| Part | + | Part | = | Whole |
|------|---|------|---|-------|
|      |   |      |   |       |

| Part | + | Part | = | Whole |
|------|---|------|---|-------|
|      |   |      |   |       |

1. Please cover the white portions of the two hexagons labeled "part" with the fewest possible congruent tiles. These are the addends.
2. Place the names of the addends into the sentence.
3. Move both addends into the hexagon labeled "whole."
4. Enter the sum into the sentence.

# Fraction Action 36

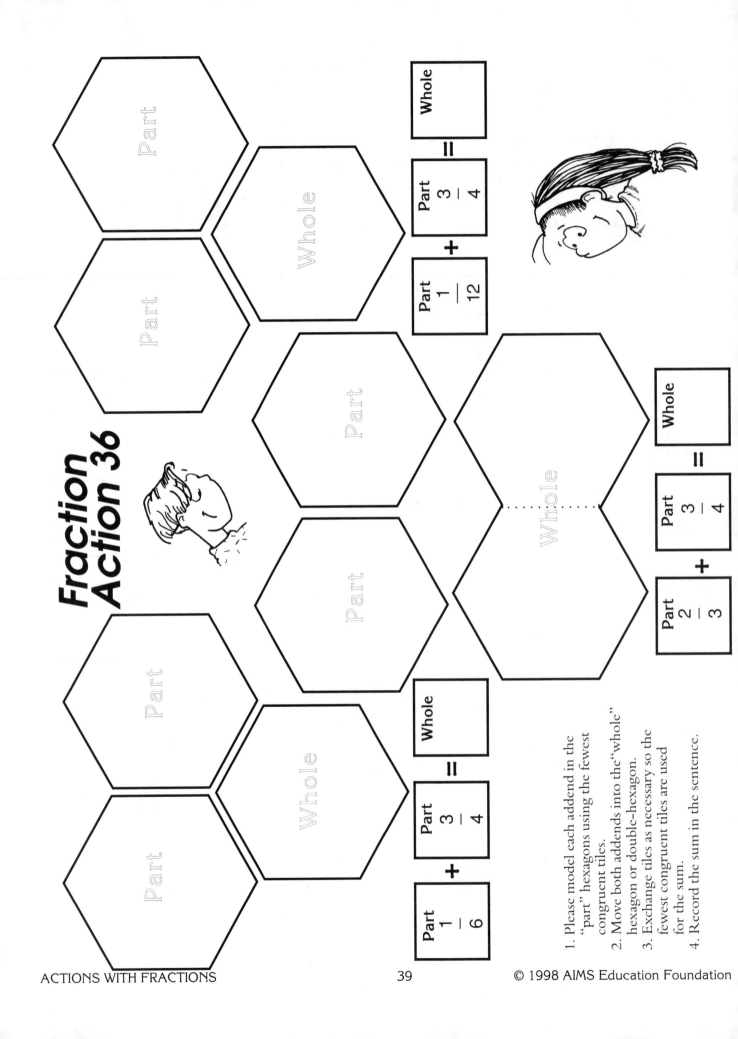

Part

Part

Whole

Part

Part

Whole

| Part | | Whole |
|---|---|---|
| $\dfrac{1}{12}$ | + $\dfrac{3}{4}$ | = |

Part

Part

Whole

| Part | | Whole |
|---|---|---|
| $\dfrac{2}{3}$ | + $\dfrac{3}{4}$ | = |

Part

Part

Whole

| Part | | Whole |
|---|---|---|
| $\dfrac{1}{6}$ | + $\dfrac{3}{4}$ | = |

1. Please model each addend in the "part" hexagons using the fewest congruent tiles.
2. Move both addends into the "whole" hexagon or double-hexagon.
3. Exchange tiles as necessary so the fewest congruent tiles are used for the sum.
4. Record the sum in the sentence.

ACTIONS WITH FRACTIONS

39

© 1998 AIMS Education Foundation

# Fraction Action 37

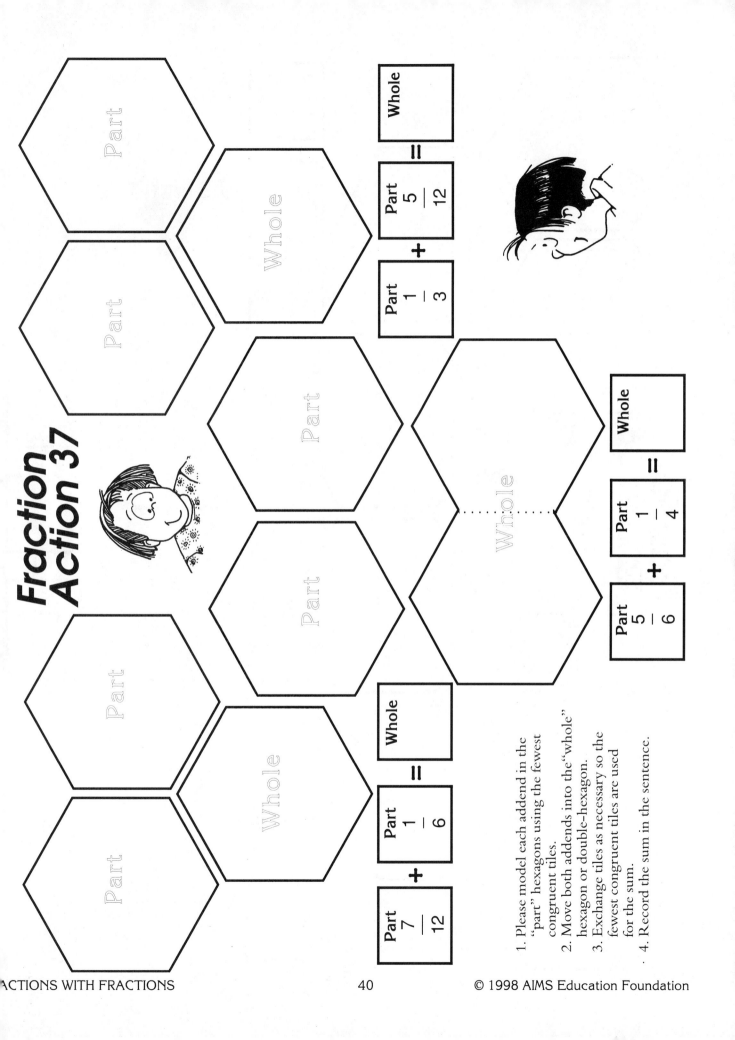

Part | Part

Whole

$$\boxed{\begin{array}{c}\text{Part} \\ \dfrac{1}{3}\end{array}} + \boxed{\begin{array}{c}\text{Part} \\ \dfrac{5}{12}\end{array}} = \boxed{\begin{array}{c}\text{Whole} \\ \\ \end{array}}$$

Part

Part

Part

Whole

$$\boxed{\begin{array}{c}\text{Part} \\ \dfrac{5}{6}\end{array}} + \boxed{\begin{array}{c}\text{Part} \\ \dfrac{1}{4}\end{array}} = \boxed{\begin{array}{c}\text{Whole} \\ \\ \end{array}}$$

Part | Part

Whole

$$\boxed{\begin{array}{c}\text{Part} \\ \dfrac{7}{12}\end{array}} + \boxed{\begin{array}{c}\text{Part} \\ \dfrac{1}{6}\end{array}} = \boxed{\begin{array}{c}\text{Whole} \\ \\ \end{array}}$$

1. Please model each addend in the "part" hexagons using the fewest congruent tiles.
2. Move both addends into the "whole" hexagon or double-hexagon.
3. Exchange tiles as necessary so the fewest congruent tiles are used for the sum.
4. Record the sum in the sentence.

# Fraction Action 38

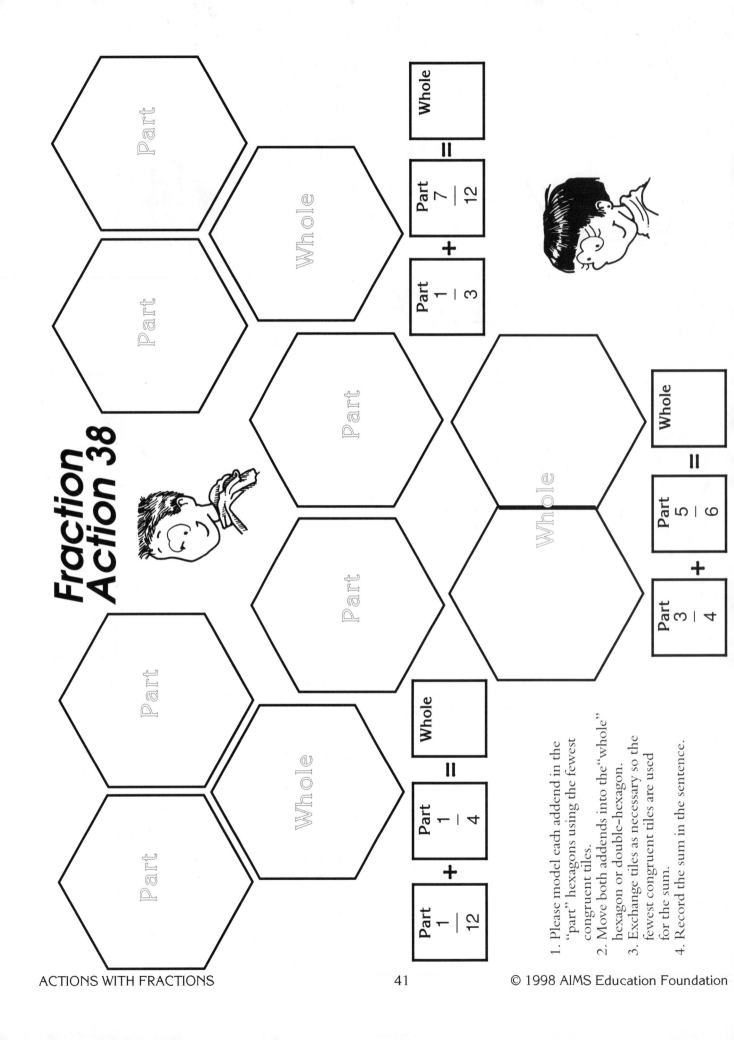

Part

Part

Whole

Part

Part

Whole

Part

Part

Whole

| Part | | Part | | Whole |
|---|---|---|---|---|
| $\dfrac{1}{3}$ | + | $\dfrac{7}{12}$ | = | |

| Part | | Part | | Whole |
|---|---|---|---|---|
| $\dfrac{3}{4}$ | + | $\dfrac{5}{6}$ | = | |

| Part | | Part | | Whole |
|---|---|---|---|---|
| $\dfrac{1}{12}$ | + | $\dfrac{1}{4}$ | = | |

1. Please model each addend in the "part" hexagons using the fewest congruent tiles.
2. Move both addends into the "whole" hexagon or double-hexagon.
3. Exchange tiles as necessary so the fewest congruent tiles are used for the sum.
4. Record the sum in the sentence.

# Fraction Action 39

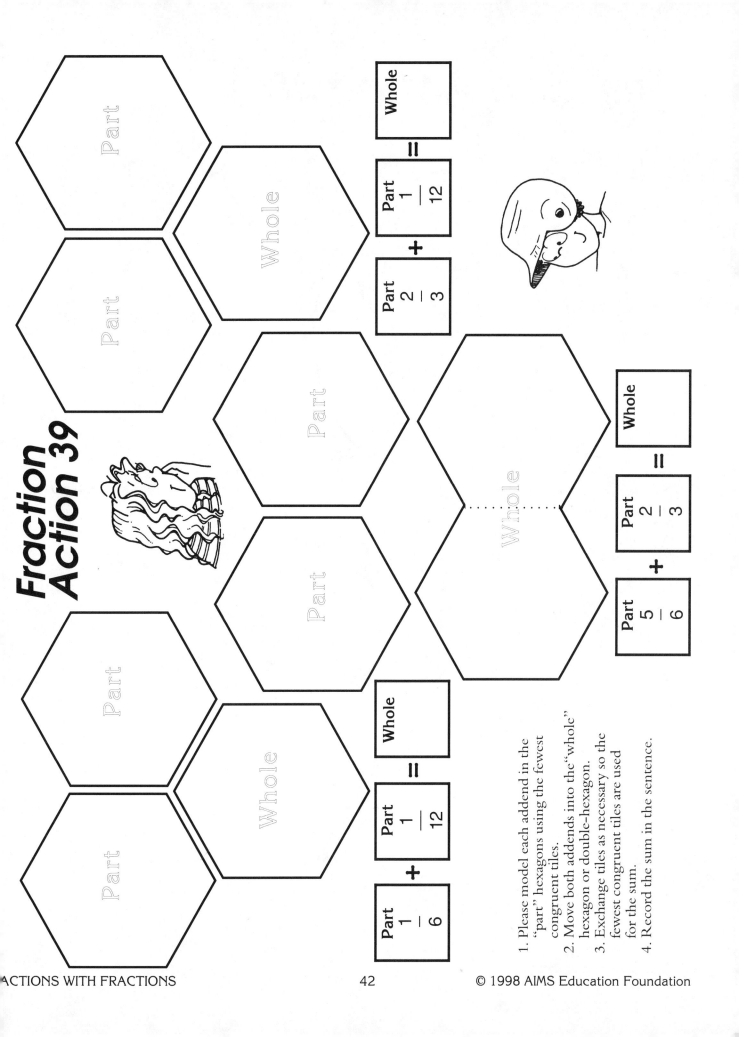

Part

Part

Whole

| Part $\frac{2}{3}$ | + | Part $\frac{1}{12}$ | = | Whole |
|---|---|---|---|---|

Part

Part

Whole

| Part $\frac{1}{6}$ | + | Part $\frac{1}{12}$ | = | Whole |
|---|---|---|---|---|

Part

Part

Whole

| Part $\frac{5}{6}$ | + | Part $\frac{2}{3}$ | = | Whole |
|---|---|---|---|---|

1. Please model each addend in the "part" hexagons using the fewest congruent tiles.
2. Move both addends into the "whole" hexagon or double-hexagon.
3. Exchange tiles as necessary so the fewest congruent tiles are used for the sum.
4. Record the sum in the sentence.

# Fraction Action 40

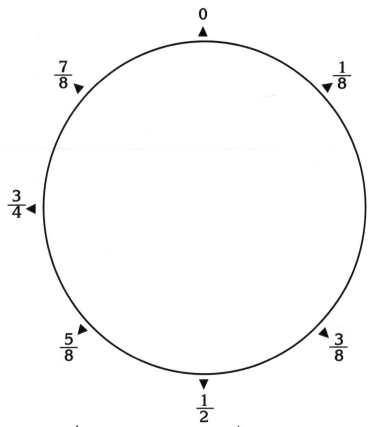

1. Please try to build mental images of the sectors representing the fractions.
2. Using these images please add the fractions mentally.
3. To add, place the first addend into the circle so it begins at zero and extends clockwise. Continue clockwise with the second hand.
4. Read the sum off the clock. Sums greater than one will pass 12 o'clock.

1.  $\dfrac{1}{2}$
    $\dfrac{1}{4}$
    ___

2.  $\dfrac{1}{8}$
    $\dfrac{1}{2}$
    ___

3.  $\dfrac{3}{8}$
    $\dfrac{1}{4}$
    ___

4.  $\dfrac{3}{4}$
    $\dfrac{1}{8}$
    ___

5.  $\dfrac{3}{8}$
    $\dfrac{1}{2}$
    ___

6.  $\dfrac{1}{4}$
    $\dfrac{2}{8}$
    ___

7.  $\dfrac{2}{4}$
    $\dfrac{1}{2}$
    ___

8.  $\dfrac{4}{8}$
    $\dfrac{1}{4}$
    ___

9.  $\dfrac{1}{4}$
    $\dfrac{1}{8}$
    ___

10. $\dfrac{1}{2}$
    $\dfrac{2}{8}$
    ___

11. $\dfrac{3}{4}$
    $\dfrac{2}{8}$
    ___

12. $\dfrac{1}{2}$
    $\dfrac{4}{8}$
    ___

# Fraction Action 41

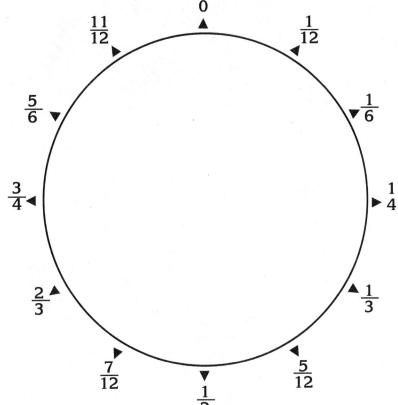

**Clock-WISE Fractions**

1. Please try to build mental images of the sectors representing the fractions.
2. Using these images please add the fractions mentally.
3. To add, place the first addend into the circle so it begins at zero and extends clockwise. Continue clockwise with the second hand.
4. Read the sum off the clock. Sums greater than one will pass 12 o'clock.

1.  $\dfrac{1}{2}$
    $\dfrac{1}{2}$
    _____

2.  $\dfrac{1}{3}$
    $\dfrac{1}{3}$
    _____

3.  $\dfrac{2}{4}$
    $\dfrac{1}{4}$
    _____

4.  $\dfrac{2}{6}$
    $\dfrac{1}{6}$
    _____

5.  $\dfrac{3}{4}$
    $\dfrac{1}{4}$
    _____

6.  $\dfrac{2}{4}$
    $\dfrac{2}{4}$
    _____

7.  $\dfrac{4}{6}$
    $\dfrac{2}{6}$
    _____

8.  $\dfrac{1}{4}$
    $\dfrac{1}{4}$
    _____

9.  $\dfrac{3}{6}$
    $\dfrac{2}{6}$
    _____

10. $\dfrac{2}{3}$
    $\dfrac{1}{3}$
    _____

11. $\dfrac{3}{6}$
    $\dfrac{1}{6}$
    _____

12. $\dfrac{3}{6}$
    $\dfrac{3}{6}$
    _____

# Fraction Action 42

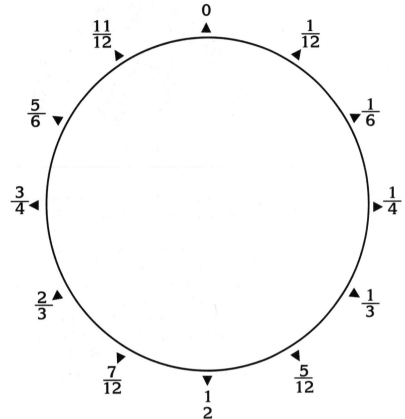

Clock-WISE Fractions

1. Please try to build mental images of the sectors representing the fractions.
2. Using these images please add the fractions mentally.
3. To add, place the first addend into the circle so it begins at zero and extends clockwise. Continue clockwise with the second hand.
4. Read the sum off the clock. Sums greater than one will pass 12 o'clock.

1. $\dfrac{1}{2}$
   $\dfrac{1}{3}$

2. $\dfrac{1}{6}$
   $\dfrac{1}{2}$

3. $\dfrac{1}{3}$
   $\dfrac{2}{4}$

4. $\dfrac{1}{3}$
   $\dfrac{1}{6}$

5. $\dfrac{1}{4}$
   $\dfrac{1}{3}$

6. $\dfrac{2}{3}$
   $\dfrac{1}{2}$

7. $\dfrac{2}{3}$
   $\dfrac{1}{4}$

8. $\dfrac{4}{6}$
   $\dfrac{1}{4}$

9. $\dfrac{2}{6}$
   $\dfrac{1}{3}$

10. $\dfrac{1}{4}$
    $\dfrac{3}{6}$

11. $\dfrac{1}{2}$
    $\dfrac{2}{6}$

12. $\dfrac{3}{4}$
    $\dfrac{1}{6}$

# Fraction Action 43

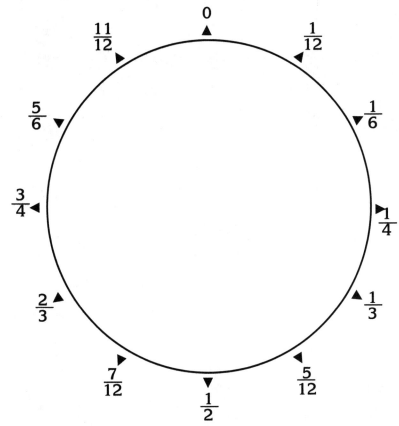

Clock-WISE Fractions

1. Please try to build mental images of the sectors representing the fractions.
2. Using these images please add the fractions mentally.
3. To add, place the first addend into the circle so it begins at zero and extends clockwise. Continue clockwise with the second hand.
4. Read the sum off the clock. Sums greater than one will pass 12 o'clock.

1.  $\dfrac{1}{2}$
    $\dfrac{3}{4}$
    _____

2.  $\dfrac{5}{6}$
    $\dfrac{1}{2}$
    _____

3.  $\dfrac{3}{4}$
    $\dfrac{1}{3}$
    _____

4.  $\dfrac{5}{6}$
    $\dfrac{1}{3}$
    _____

5.  $\dfrac{2}{3}$
    $\dfrac{2}{3}$
    _____

6.  $\dfrac{2}{4}$
    $\dfrac{3}{4}$
    _____

7.  $\dfrac{3}{4}$
    $\dfrac{2}{3}$
    _____

8.  $\dfrac{3}{4}$
    $\dfrac{3}{4}$
    _____

9.  $\dfrac{2}{3}$
    $\dfrac{2}{4}$
    _____

10. $\dfrac{1}{6}$
    $\dfrac{2}{3}$
    _____

11. $\dfrac{1}{4}$
    $\dfrac{5}{6}$
    _____

12. $\dfrac{2}{3}$
    $\dfrac{5}{6}$
    _____

# Fraction Action 44

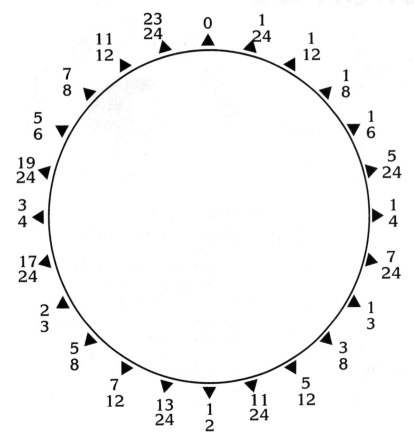

*Clock-WISE Fractions*

1. Please try to build mental images of the sectors representing the fractions.
2. Using these images please add the fractions mentally.
3. To add, place the first addend into the circle so it begins at zero and extends clockwise. Continue clockwise with the second hand.
4. Read the sum off the clock. Sums greater than one will pass 12 -o'clock.

1.  $\dfrac{1}{2}$
    $\dfrac{5}{8}$

2.  $\dfrac{2}{3}$
    $\dfrac{7}{8}$

3.  $\dfrac{1}{3}$
    $\dfrac{1}{8}$

4.  $\dfrac{1}{4}$
    $\dfrac{5}{8}$

5.  $\dfrac{5}{8}$
    $\dfrac{2}{3}$

6.  $\dfrac{1}{3}$
    $\dfrac{5}{8}$

7.  $\dfrac{7}{8}$
    $\dfrac{1}{2}$

8.  $\dfrac{3}{8}$
    $\dfrac{2}{3}$

9.  $\dfrac{3}{8}$
    $\dfrac{1}{3}$

10. $\dfrac{2}{3}$
    $\dfrac{1}{8}$

11. $\dfrac{3}{4}$
    $\dfrac{5}{8}$

12. $\dfrac{7}{8}$
    $\dfrac{1}{3}$

# Fraction Action 45

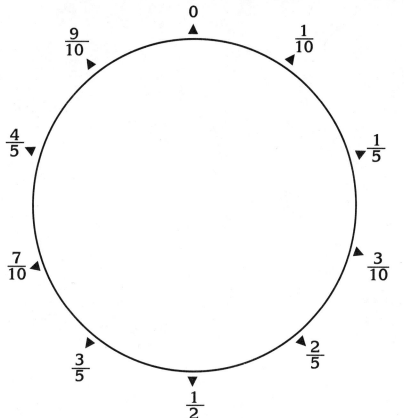

### Clock-WISE Fractions

1. Please try to build mental images of the sectors representing the fractions.
2. Using these images please add the fractions mentally.
3. To add, place the first addend into the circle so it begins at zero and extends clockwise. Continue clockwise with the second hand.
4. Read the sum off the clock. Sums greater than one will pass 12 o'clock.

1.  $\dfrac{1}{2}$
    $\dfrac{1}{5}$

2.  $\dfrac{2}{5}$
    $\dfrac{1}{2}$

3.  $\dfrac{3}{5}$
    $\dfrac{4}{5}$

4.  $\dfrac{2}{5}$
    $\dfrac{4}{5}$

5.  $\dfrac{1}{5}$
    $\dfrac{2}{5}$

6.  $\dfrac{3}{5}$
    $\dfrac{3}{5}$

7.  $\dfrac{4}{10}$
    $\dfrac{1}{2}$

8.  $\dfrac{3}{5}$
    $\dfrac{1}{2}$

9.  $\dfrac{4}{5}$
    $\dfrac{4}{5}$

10. $\dfrac{1}{2}$
    $\dfrac{4}{5}$

11. $\dfrac{3}{5}$
    $\dfrac{2}{5}$

12. $\dfrac{6}{10}$
    $\dfrac{2}{5}$

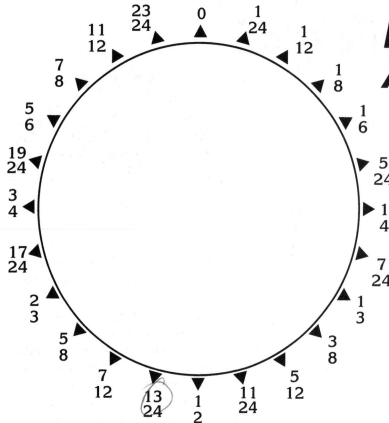

# Fraction Action 46

Please find the sums. Use sectors to check your answers.

1.  $\dfrac{1}{2}\dfrac{(4)}{(4)} + \dfrac{3}{8} + \dfrac{1}{4}\dfrac{(2)}{(2)} = \dfrac{9}{24}$

2.  $\dfrac{3}{4} + \dfrac{1}{8} + \dfrac{1}{3} =$

3.  $\dfrac{1}{6} + \dfrac{3}{8} + \dfrac{2}{3} =$

4.  $\dfrac{5}{6} + \dfrac{1}{8} + \dfrac{3}{4} =$

5.  $\dfrac{7}{8} + \dfrac{1}{(4)\,2} + \dfrac{1}{4} = \dfrac{13}{24}$

6.  $\dfrac{1}{3} + \dfrac{7}{8} + \dfrac{1}{6} =$

7.  $\dfrac{5}{8} + \dfrac{3}{4} + \dfrac{1}{2} =$

8.  $\dfrac{1}{2} + \dfrac{3}{8} + \dfrac{2}{3} =$

9.  $\dfrac{3}{4} + \dfrac{7}{8} + \dfrac{1}{2} =$

10. $\dfrac{1}{8} + \dfrac{1}{6} + \dfrac{1}{4} =$

11. $\dfrac{5}{6} + \dfrac{1}{4} + \dfrac{3}{8} =$

12. $\dfrac{2}{3} + \dfrac{7}{8} + \dfrac{1}{4} =$

13. $\dfrac{5}{8}\dfrac{15}{(3)} + \dfrac{1}{4}\dfrac{6}{} + \dfrac{1}{3}\dfrac{8}{} = \dfrac{}{24}$

14. $\dfrac{7}{8} + \dfrac{3}{4} + \dfrac{2}{3} =$

# Fraction Action 47

Please use one color for the shaded part of the left circle and another color for the shaded part of the center circle. Use the same colors to show the sum. Then name the fractions and complete the sentences.

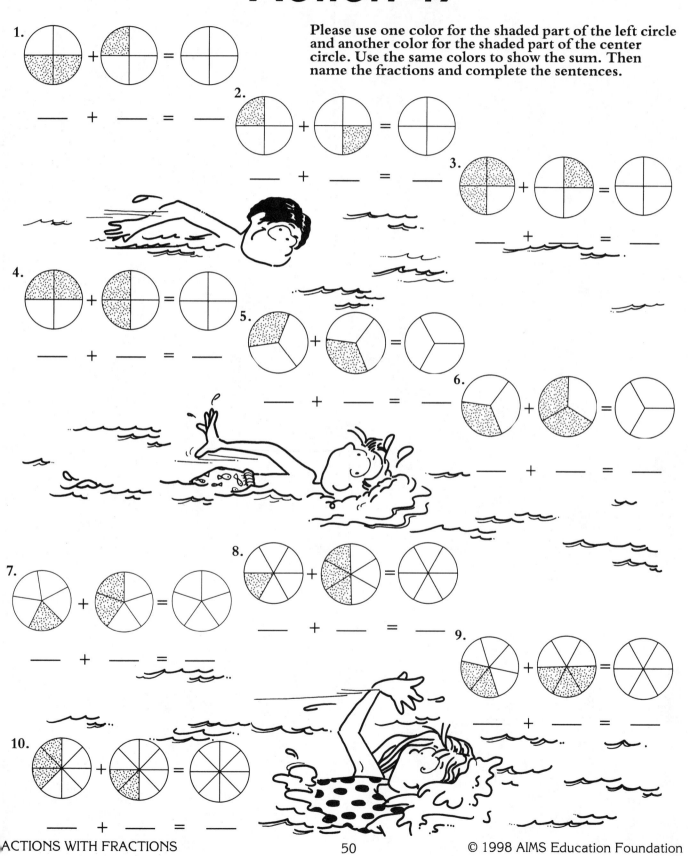

1. ⬕ + ⬕ = ⬕

___ + ___ = ___

2. ⬕ + ⬕ = ⬕

___ + ___ = ___

3. ⬕ + ⬕ = ⬕

___ + ___ = ___.

4. ⬕ + ⬕ = ⬕

___ + ___ = ___

5. ⬙ + ⬙ = ⬙

___ + ___ = ___

6. ⬙ + ⬙ = ⬙

___ + ___ = ___

7. ⬙ + ⬙ = ⬙

___ + ___ = ___

8. ⬡ + ⬡ = ⬡

___ + ___ = ___

9. ⬡ + ⬡ = ⬡

___ + ___ = ___.

10. ⊛ + ⊛ = ⊛

___ + ___ = ___

# Fraction Action 48

Please use one color for the shaded part of the left circle and another color for the shaded part of the center circle. Use the same colors to show the sum. Then name the fractions and complete the sentence.

# Fraction
# Action 49

Please color the first part red and the
second part green. Then find the sum
and complete the sentence.

1.

$$\frac{1}{3} + \frac{1}{2} = \frac{5}{6}$$

2.

$$\frac{3}{4}{}^{2} + \frac{1}{8} = \frac{7}{8}$$

3.

$$\frac{2}{3}{}^{4} + \frac{1}{4} = \frac{11}{12}$$

4.

$$\frac{1}{6} + \frac{1}{2}{}^{3} = \frac{4}{6} \quad \frac{2}{3}$$

5.

$$\frac{2}{3} + \frac{1}{6} = \underline{\quad}$$

6.

$$\frac{3}{4} + \frac{1}{6} = \underline{\quad}$$

7.

$$\frac{1}{2} + \frac{1}{4} = \underline{\quad}$$

8.

$$\frac{2}{5} + \frac{1}{3} = \underline{\quad}$$

ACTIONS WITH FRACTIONS            52            © 1998 AIMS Education Foundation

# Fraction
# Action 50

Please color part of the circle red and part green, always leaving some part uncolored. Write a sentence naming the three fractional numbers in lowest terms, — + — = —, in which the first fraction names the red part, the second the green part, and the third is their sum.

1.

—— + —— = ——

2.

—— + —— = ——

3.

—— + —— = ——

4.

—— + —— = ——

5.

—— + —— = ——

6.

—— + —— = ——

7.

—— + —— = ——

8.

—— + —— = ——

9.

—— + —— = ——

10.

—— + —— = ——

11.

—— + —— = ——

12.

—— + —— = ——

13.

—— + —— = ——

14.

—— + —— = ——

15.

—— + —— = ——

# Fraction Action 51

Please find the sum for each of the following.
Check your answer using the fraction ruler.

1.  $\dfrac{1}{2}$
    $\dfrac{1}{4}$
    ⎯⎯

2.  $\dfrac{3}{4}$
    $\dfrac{2}{3}$
    ⎯⎯

3.  $\dfrac{2}{3}$
    $\dfrac{5}{6}$
    ⎯⎯

4.  $\dfrac{5}{6}$
    $\dfrac{1}{4}$
    ⎯⎯

5.  $\dfrac{3}{4}$
    $\dfrac{1}{2}$
    ⎯⎯

6.  $\dfrac{2}{3}$
    $\dfrac{1}{6}$
    ⎯⎯

7.  $\dfrac{5}{6}$
    $\dfrac{1}{3}$
    ⎯⎯

8.  $\dfrac{1}{3}$
    $\dfrac{3}{4}$
    ⎯⎯

9.  $\dfrac{3}{4}$
    $\dfrac{5}{6}$
    ⎯⎯

10. $\dfrac{5}{12}$
    $\dfrac{2}{3}$
    ⎯⎯

11. $\dfrac{2}{3}$
    $\dfrac{1}{2}$
    ⎯⎯

12. $\dfrac{1}{4}$
    $\dfrac{2}{3}$
    ⎯⎯

13. $\dfrac{5}{6}$
    $\dfrac{5}{12}$
    ⎯⎯

14. $\dfrac{3}{4}$
    $\dfrac{7}{12}$
    ⎯⎯

15. $\dfrac{1}{3}$
    $\dfrac{1}{2}$
    ⎯⎯

16. $\dfrac{7}{12}$
    $\dfrac{3}{4}$
    ⎯⎯

The fraction ruler (left side) shows the following markings:

**Upper section (from 2 down to 1):**
2
$\frac{23}{24}$
$\frac{11}{12}$
$\frac{7}{8}$
$\frac{5}{6}$
$\frac{19}{24}$
$\frac{3}{4}$
$\frac{17}{24}$
$\frac{2}{3}$
$\frac{5}{8}$
$\frac{7}{12}$
$\frac{13}{24}$
$\frac{1}{2}$
$\frac{11}{24}$
$\frac{5}{12}$
$\frac{3}{8}$
$\frac{1}{3}$
$\frac{7}{24}$
$\frac{1}{4}$
$\frac{5}{24}$
$\frac{1}{6}$
$\frac{1}{8}$
$\frac{1}{12}$
$\frac{1}{24}$
1

**Lower section (from 1 down):**
$\frac{23}{24}$
$\frac{11}{12}$
$\frac{7}{8}$
$\frac{5}{6}$
$\frac{19}{24}$
$\frac{3}{4}$
$\frac{17}{24}$
$\frac{2}{3}$
$\frac{5}{8}$
$\frac{7}{12}$
$\frac{13}{24}$
$\frac{1}{2}$
$\frac{11}{24}$
$\frac{5}{12}$
$\frac{3}{8}$
$\frac{1}{3}$
$\frac{7}{24}$
$\frac{1}{4}$
$\frac{5}{24}$
$\frac{1}{6}$
$\frac{1}{8}$
$\frac{1}{12}$
$\frac{1}{24}$

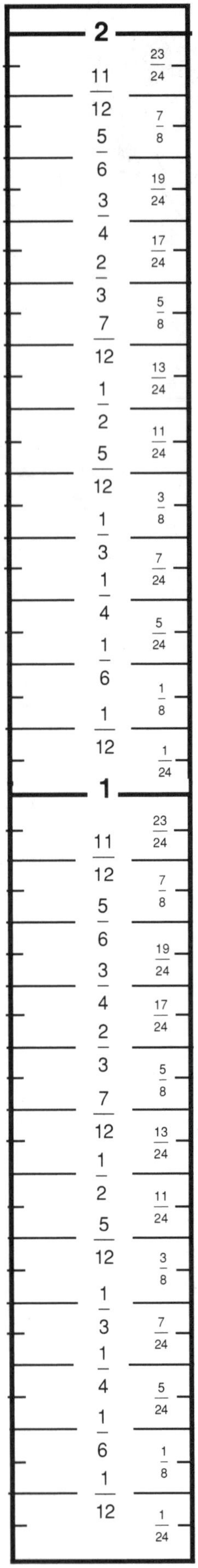
2
23/24
11/12
7/8
5/6
19/24
3/4
17/24
2/3
5/8
7/12
13/24
1/2
11/24
5/12
3/8
1/3
7/24
1/4
5/24
1/6
1/8
1/12
1/24
1
23/24
11/12
7/8
5/6
19/24
3/4
17/24
2/3
5/8
7/12
13/24
1/2
11/24
5/12
3/8
1/3
7/24
1/4
5/24
1/6
1/8
1/12
1/24

# Fraction Action 52

**Please find the sum for each of the following. Check your answer using the fraction ruler.**

1. $1\frac{1}{2} + \frac{7}{8}$

2. $1\frac{3}{4} + \frac{2}{3}$

3. $2\frac{1}{2} + 1\frac{3}{8}$

4. $1\frac{1}{3} + \frac{3}{4}$

5. $1\frac{2}{3} + 1\frac{5}{8}$

6. $1\frac{1}{4} + 2\frac{1}{3}$

7. $2\frac{3}{8} + 1\frac{1}{4}$

8. $1\frac{1}{2} + \frac{3}{8}$

9. $1\frac{1}{8} + 1\frac{1}{3}$

10. $2\frac{5}{8} + \frac{5}{6}$

11. $1\frac{5}{6} + 1\frac{1}{8}$

12. $1\frac{1}{6} + \frac{7}{8}$

13. $\frac{7}{8} + \frac{5}{6}$

14. $1\frac{1}{6} + 2\frac{1}{4}$

15. $1\frac{3}{8} + \frac{5}{6}$

16. $1\frac{2}{3} + 2\frac{1}{6}$

 

# Fraction Action 53

Please match each picture to a
sentence below. Then complete
the sentence.

A     B     C

D     E     F     G

H     I     J     K     L     M

N     O     P

1. ◯ $\dfrac{3}{12} + \dfrac{5}{12} = -$

2. ◯ $\dfrac{1}{4} + \dfrac{2}{4} = -$

3. ◯ $\dfrac{3}{10} + \dfrac{4}{10} = -$

4. ◯ $\dfrac{5}{8} + \dfrac{3}{8} = -$

5. ◯ $\dfrac{1}{5} + \dfrac{2}{5} = -$

6. ◯ $\dfrac{2}{10} + \dfrac{5}{10} = -$

7. ◯ $\dfrac{2}{9} + \dfrac{4}{9} = -$

8. ◯ $\dfrac{1}{3} + \dfrac{1}{3} = -$

9. ◯ $\dfrac{3}{9} + \dfrac{4}{9} = -$

10. ◯ $\dfrac{1}{4} + \dfrac{3}{4} = -$

11. ◯ $\dfrac{2}{6} + \dfrac{3}{6} = -$

12. ◯ $\dfrac{4}{6} + \dfrac{1}{6} = -$

13. ◯ $\dfrac{3}{8} + \dfrac{2}{8} = -$

14. ◯ $\dfrac{7}{12} + \dfrac{2}{12} = -$

15. ◯ $\dfrac{1}{4} + \dfrac{1}{4} = -$

16. ◯ $\dfrac{5}{8} + \dfrac{1}{8} = -$

# Part 4

## Whole – Part = Part
## Subtraction of Fractions

The approach to subtraction used here is whole – part = part. In *Fraction Action 54 – 63,* hexagonal tiles are used. Several options are possible: problems may first be solved either mentally or using the standard algorithm and the solutions checked using the manipulative model; or, the solution can be arrived at the manipulative level and the results used to complete the sentence.

In *Fraction Action 54 – 58,* the whole (minuend) and one part (subtrahend) are represented. The whole is to be separated into two parts: the magnitude of the first part is shown with the second part to be determined by the remainder. The process is outlined in the directions. The whole and both parts are to be identified and used to complete the sentence. *Whole* here is used to mean the amount available at the outset.

The inverse process is used in *Fraction Action 59 – 63.* The whole is named and is to be modeled with hexagonal tiles. The indicated part is separated out from the whole and moved into a *part* space, exchanging tiles as appropriate. The remainder, representing the difference, is moved into the second part space. The difference is determined from the model by identifying the content of the second part space.

In *Fraction Action 64 – 66,* pie slices are used to model the fractional parts. In this approach to subtraction, the whole or beginning amount is represented by a pie slice or congruent pie slices (found in the *Appendix)* placed into a clock beginning at zero and moving clockwise. The first part or subtrahend is used to cover the minuend beginning at the far end and returning counterclockwise. The uncovered part models the difference.

In *Fraction Action 67,* unit bars are used to model subtraction. Note that the whole is represented in bars with an arrow pointing upward and the part to be removed in bars with an arrow pointing downward. Also, note that the zero end of the part is matched with the far end of the whole but the ruler points downward. The difference is read at the bottom of the part representation. The sentence is completed from the represented information.

The manipulative approach is used to check answers first computed in *Fraction Action 68 – 71.* The manipulation is like that in activity *67:* the whole is located on the fixed ruler and the part to be subtracted on the moveable ruler (found in the *Appendix)* The zero point of the moveable ruler is matched with the far end of the numerator on the fixed ruler with the moveable ruler pointing downward. The second difference is read on the fixed ruler at the bottom end of the subtracted part.

The *Fractions in the Pie Shop* (pages 76-80) illustrates that a more meaningful and easier algorithm can emerge in response to the question: How does the subtraction of fractions take place in real-world situations? Because of its significance, a separate explanation is given as the introduction to that activity.

# Fraction Action 54

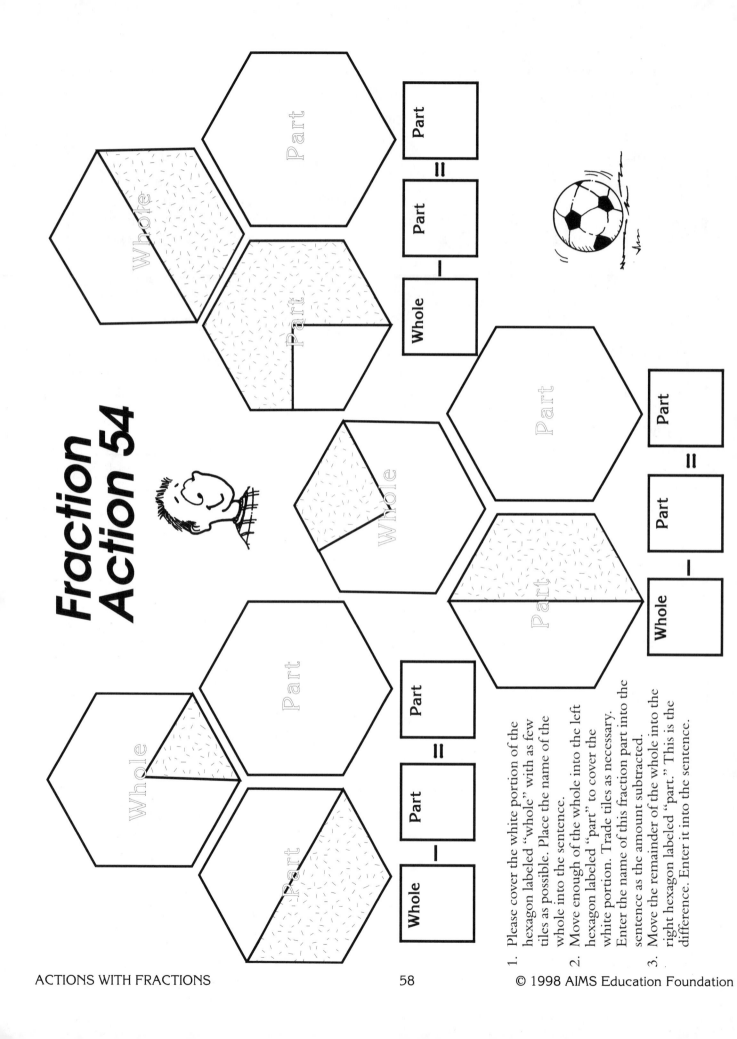

Whole — Part = Part

Whole — Part = Part

Part — Part = Part

1. Please cover the white portion of the hexagon labeled "whole" with as few tiles as possible. Place the name of the whole into the sentence.

2. Move enough of the whole into the left hexagon labeled "part" to cover the white portion. Trade tiles as necessary. Enter the name of this fraction part into the sentence as the amount subtracted.

3. Move the remainder of the whole into the right hexagon labeled "part." This is the difference. Enter it into the sentence.

# Fraction
# Action 55

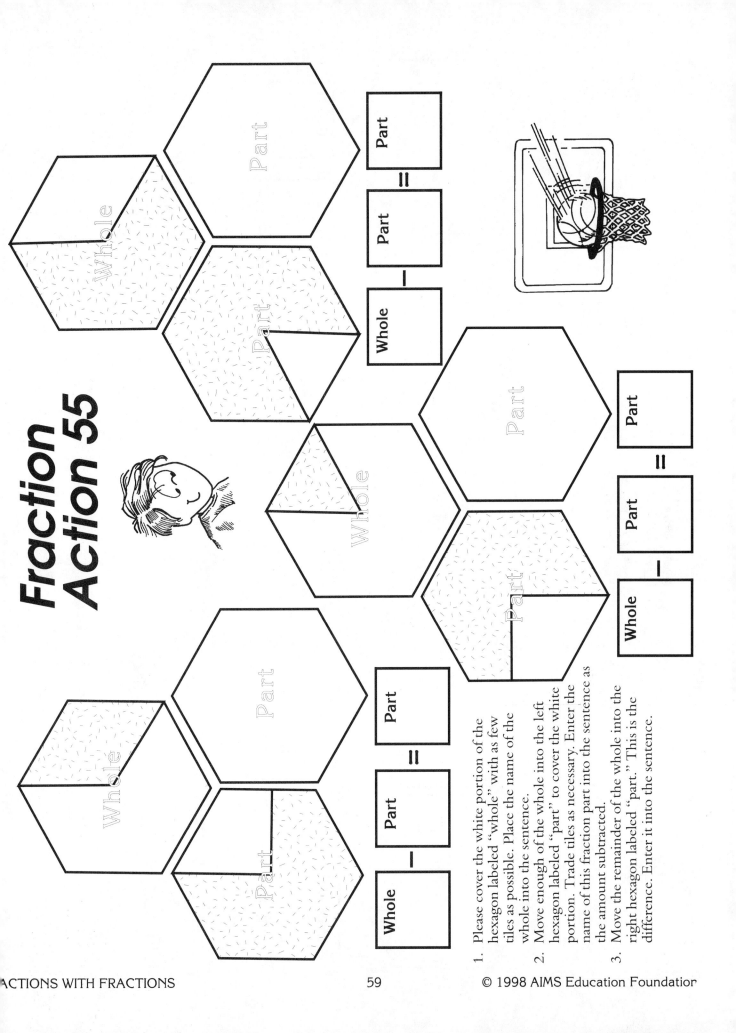

Whole

Part

Part

Whole

Part

| Part | − | Part | = | Part |

Whole

Part

Part

Whole

Part

| Whole | − | Part | = | Part |

Part

Whole

Part

| Whole | − | Part | = | Part |

1. Please cover the white portion of the hexagon labeled "whole" with as few tiles as possible. Place the name of the whole into the sentence.

2. Move enough of the whole into the left hexagon labeled "part" to cover the white portion. Trade tiles as necessary. Enter the name of this fraction part into the sentence as the amount subtracted.

3. Move the remainder of the whole into the right hexagon labeled "part." This is the difference. Enter it into the sentence.

59

# Fraction Action 56

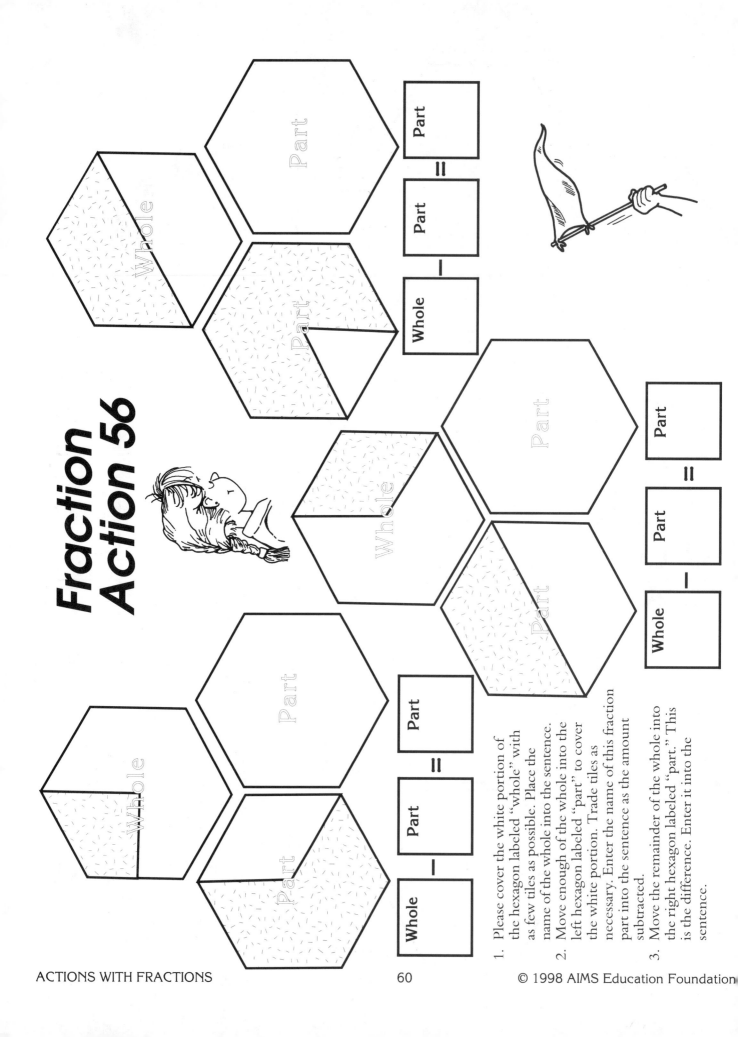

Whole — Part = Part

Whole — Part = Part

Whole — Part = Part

1. Please cover the white portion of the hexagon labeled "whole" with as few tiles as possible. Place the name of the whole into the sentence.

2. Move enough of the whole into the left hexagon labeled "part" to cover the white portion. Trade tiles as necessary. Enter the name of this fraction part into the sentence as the amount subtracted.

3. Move the remainder of the whole into the right hexagon labeled "part." This is the difference. Enter it into the sentence.

# Fraction
# Action 57

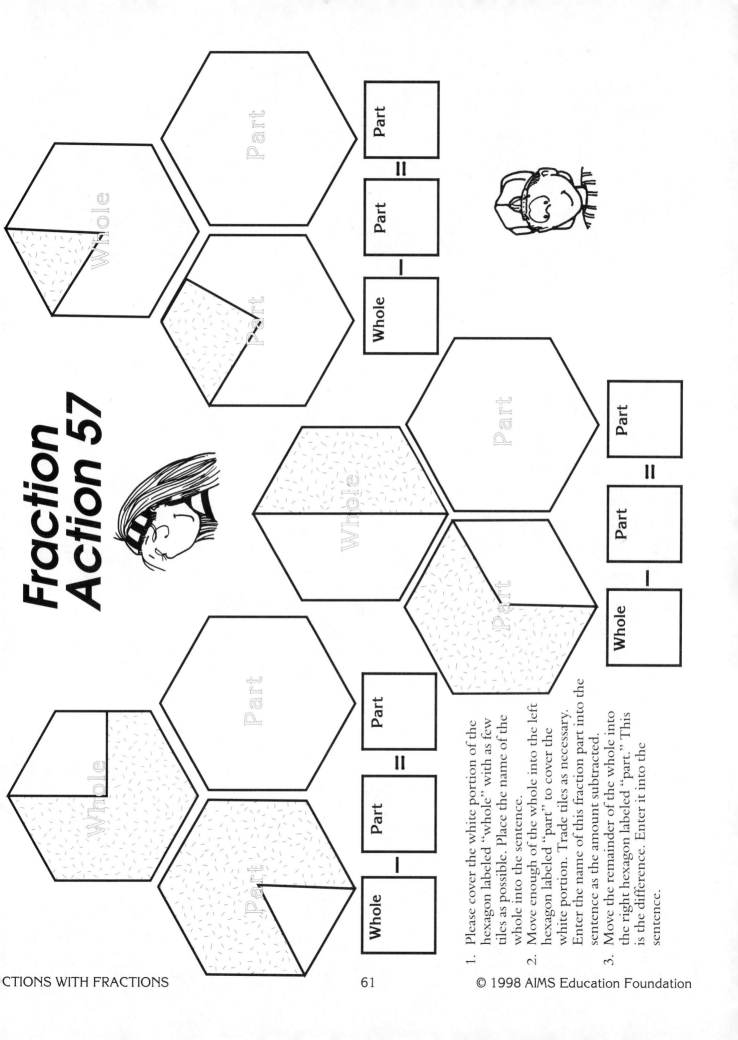

Whole

Part

Part

Whole

| Whole | – | Part | = | Part |

Whole

Part

Part

| Whole | – | Part | = | Part |

Whole

Part

Part

| Whole | – | Part | = | Part |

1. Please cover the white portion of the hexagon labeled "whole" with as few tiles as possible. Place the name of the whole into the sentence.

2. Move enough of the whole into the left hexagon labeled "part" to cover the white portion. Trade tiles as necessary. Enter the name of this fraction part into the sentence as the amount subtracted.

3. Move the remainder of the whole into the right hexagon labeled "part." This is the difference. Enter it into the sentence.

# Fraction
# Action 58

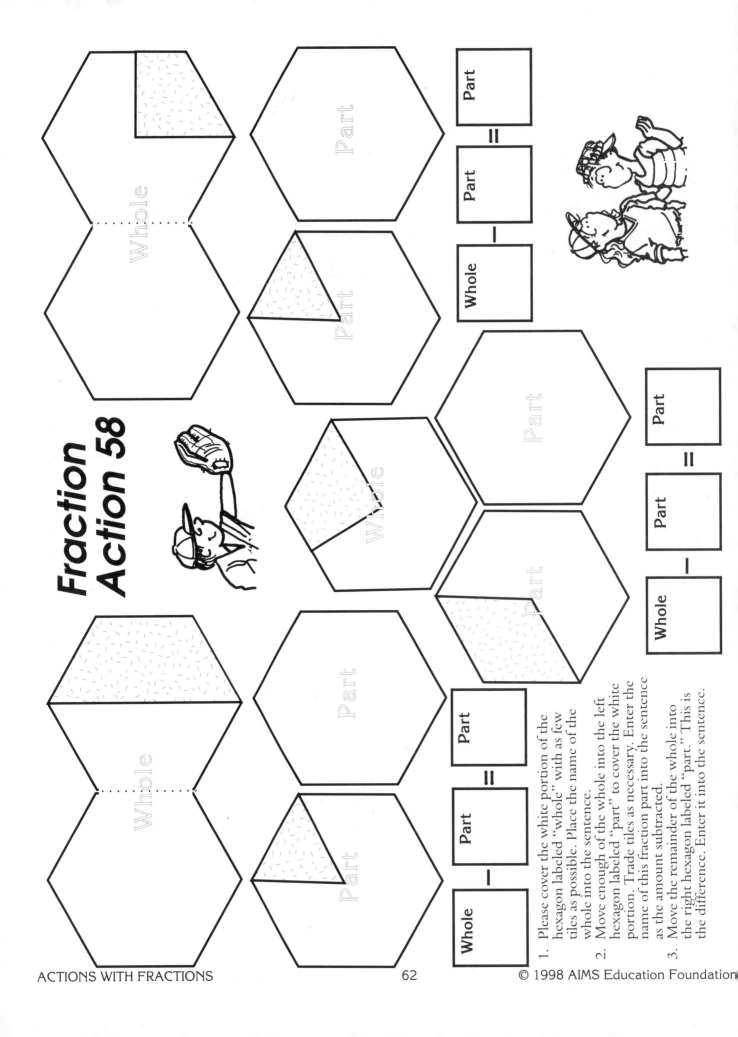

Whole

Part

Part

Part

Part

| Whole | − | Part | = | Part |

Whole

Part

Part

Part

Whole

| Whole | − | Part | = | Part |

| Whole | − | Part | = | Part |

1. Please cover the white portion of the hexagon labeled "whole" with as few tiles as possible. Place the name of the whole into the sentence.

2. Move enough of the whole into the left hexagon labeled "part" to cover the white portion. Trade tiles as necessary. Enter the name of this fraction part into the sentence as the amount subtracted.

3. Move the remainder of the whole into the right hexagon labeled "part." This is the difference. Enter it into the sentence.

# Fraction
# Action 59

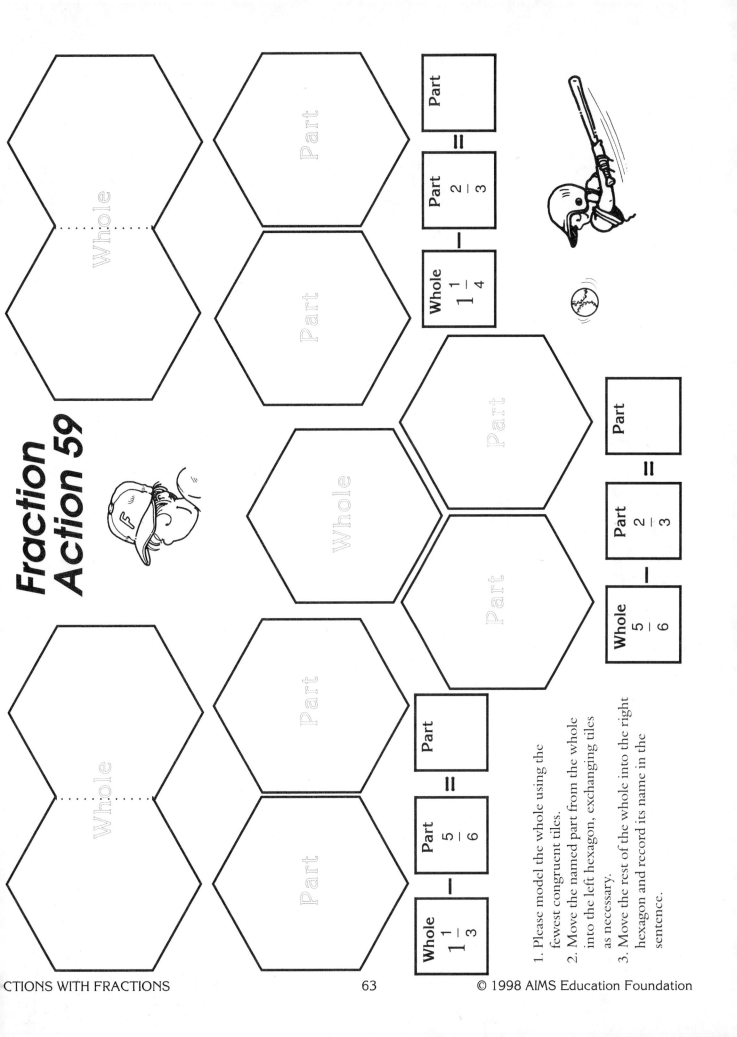

Whole

Part

Part

Part

Whole

Part

Part

Whole

Part

Part

| Whole $1\frac{1}{4}$ | − | Part $\frac{2}{3}$ | = | Part |

| Whole $\frac{5}{6}$ | − | Part $\frac{2}{3}$ | = | Part |

| Whole $1\frac{1}{3}$ | − | Part $\frac{5}{6}$ | = | Part |

1. Please model the whole using the fewest congruent tiles.
2. Move the named part from the whole into the left hexagon, exchanging tiles as necessary.
3. Move the rest of the whole into the right hexagon and record its name in the sentence.

# Fraction Action 60

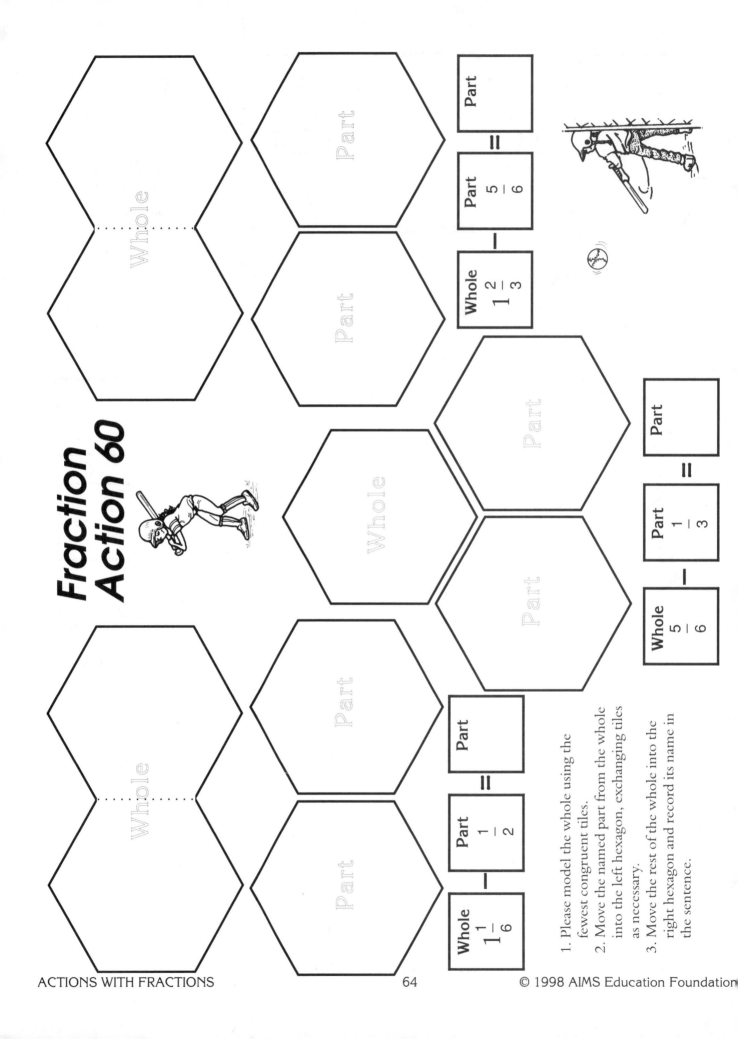

**Whole** (hexagon)

**Part** (hexagon)    **Part** (hexagon)

$$\text{Whole } 1\frac{2}{3} - \text{Part } \frac{5}{6} = \text{Part}$$

**Whole** (hexagon)    **Part** (hexagon)

**Part** (hexagon)

$$\text{Whole } \frac{5}{6} - \text{Part } \frac{1}{3} = \text{Part}$$

**Whole** (hexagon)

**Part** (hexagon)    **Part** (hexagon)

$$\text{Whole } 1\frac{1}{6} - \text{Part } \frac{1}{2} = \text{Part}$$

1. Please model the whole using the fewest congruent tiles.
2. Move the named part from the whole into the left hexagon, exchanging tiles as necessary.
3. Move the rest of the whole into the right hexagon and record its name in the sentence.

# Fraction Action 61

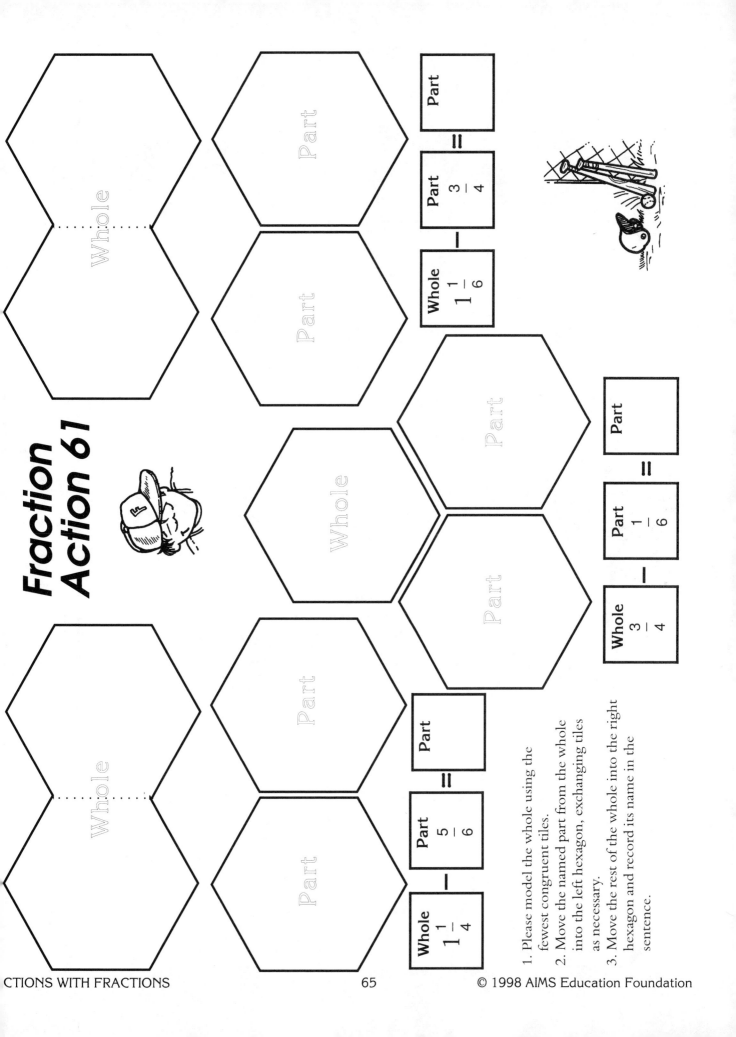

Whole

Part

Part

Part

Whole

Part

| Whole $1\frac{1}{6}$ | − | Part $\frac{3}{4}$ | = | Part |

Whole

Part

Part

| Whole $\frac{3}{4}$ | − | Part $\frac{1}{6}$ | = | Part |

Whole

Part

Part

| Whole $1\frac{1}{4}$ | − | Part $\frac{5}{6}$ | = | Part |

1. Please model the whole using the fewest congruent tiles.
2. Move the named part from the whole into the left hexagon, exchanging tiles as necessary.
3. Move the rest of the whole into the right hexagon and record its name in the sentence.

# Fraction Action 62

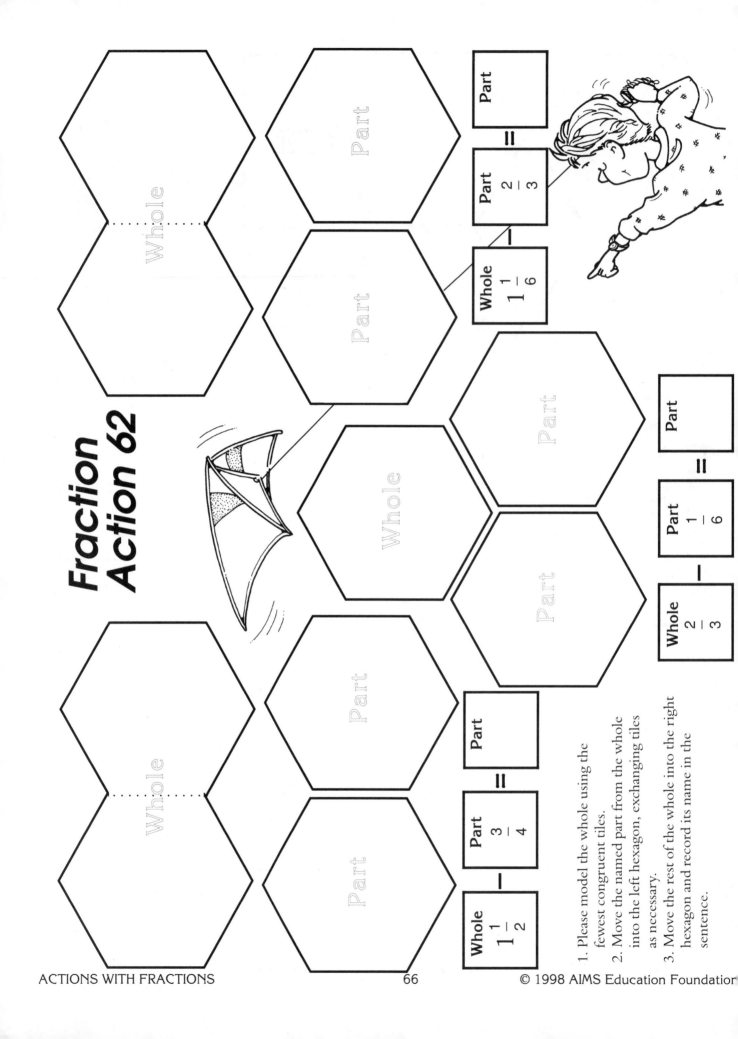

Whole

Part

Part

| Part | | Part | |
|------|---|------|---|
| Whole $1\frac{1}{6}$ | — | $\frac{2}{3}$ | = |

Whole

| Whole $\frac{2}{3}$ | — | $\frac{1}{6}$ | = | Part |
|---|---|---|---|---|

Whole

Part

Part

| Whole $1\frac{1}{2}$ | — | Part $\frac{3}{4}$ | = | Part |
|---|---|---|---|---|

1. Please model the whole using the fewest congruent tiles.
2. Move the named part from the whole into the left hexagon, exchanging tiles as necessary.
3. Move the rest of the whole into the right hexagon and record its name in the sentence.

# Fraction Action 63

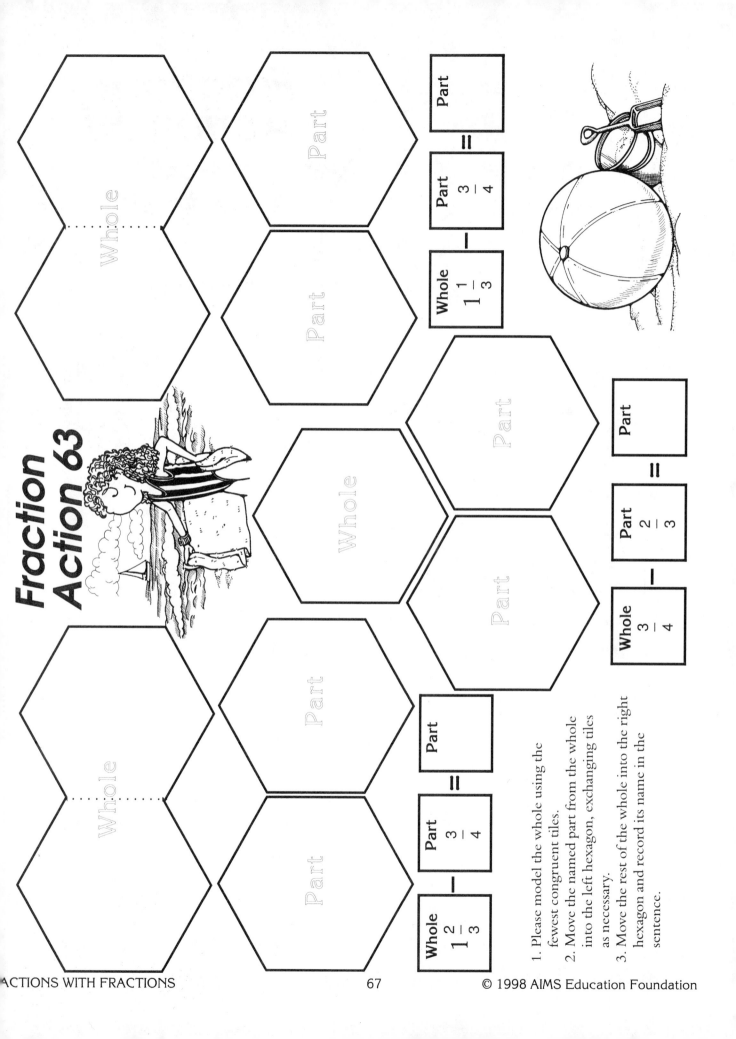

**Whole**

**Part**

**Part**

**Whole**

**Part**

**Part**

**Whole**

**Part**

**Part**

| Whole $1\frac{1}{3}$ | − | Part $\frac{3}{4}$ | = | Part |

| Whole $\frac{3}{4}$ | − | Part $\frac{2}{3}$ | = | Part |

| Whole $1\frac{2}{3}$ | − | Part $\frac{3}{4}$ | = | Part |

1. Please model the whole using the fewest congruent tiles.

2. Move the named part from the whole into the left hexagon, exchanging tiles as necessary.

3. Move the rest of the whole into the right hexagon and record its name in the sentence.

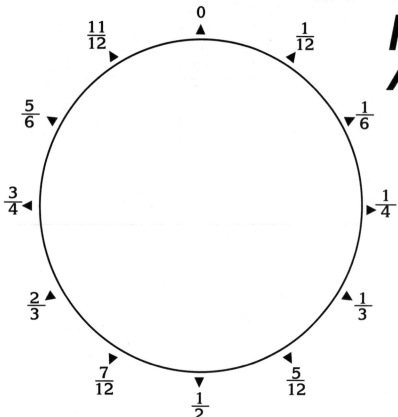

0

$\frac{11}{12}$

$\frac{1}{12}$

$\frac{5}{6}$

$\frac{1}{6}$

$\frac{3}{4}$

$\frac{1}{4}$

$\frac{2}{3}$

$\frac{1}{3}$

$\frac{7}{12}$

$\frac{5}{12}$

$\frac{1}{2}$

# Fraction Action 64

Please find the differences.
Use sectors to check your answers

1.  $\frac{2}{3}$
    $-\frac{1}{2}$

2.  $\frac{3}{4}$
    $-\frac{1}{3}$

3.  $\frac{2}{3}$
    $-\frac{1}{4}$

4.  $\frac{3}{4}$
    $-\frac{2}{3}$

5.  $\frac{1}{2}$
    $-\frac{1}{3}$

6.  $\frac{5}{6}$
    $-\frac{1}{4}$

7.  $\frac{5}{6}$
    $-\frac{1}{3}$

8.  $\frac{1}{2}$
    $-\frac{1}{6}$

9.  $\frac{5}{6}$
    $-\frac{2}{3}$

10. $\frac{3}{4}$
    $-\frac{1}{6}$

11. $\frac{1}{2}$
    $-\frac{1}{4}$

12. $\frac{5}{6}$
    $-\frac{3}{4}$

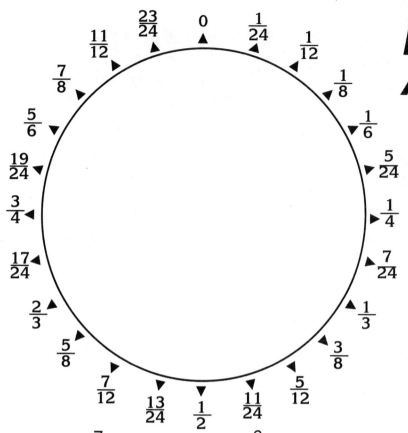

$$\frac{23}{24} \quad 0 \quad \frac{1}{24}$$

$$\frac{11}{12} \qquad \frac{1}{12}$$

$$\frac{7}{8} \qquad\qquad \frac{1}{8}$$

$$\frac{5}{6} \qquad\qquad \frac{1}{6}$$

$$\frac{19}{24} \qquad\qquad \frac{5}{24}$$

$$\frac{3}{4} \qquad\qquad \frac{1}{4}$$

$$\frac{17}{24} \qquad\qquad \frac{7}{24}$$

$$\frac{2}{3} \qquad\qquad \frac{1}{3}$$

$$\frac{5}{8} \qquad\qquad \frac{3}{8}$$

$$\frac{7}{12} \quad \frac{13}{24} \quad \frac{1}{2} \quad \frac{11}{24} \quad \frac{5}{12}$$

# Fraction Action 65

Please find the differences.
Use sectors to check your answers

1. $\dfrac{7}{8}$  $-\dfrac{1}{2}$ _____

2. $\dfrac{6}{8}$  $-\dfrac{1}{4}$ _____

3. $\dfrac{5}{6}$  $-\dfrac{1}{4}$ _____

4. $\dfrac{3}{4}$  $-\dfrac{2}{3}$ _____

5. $\dfrac{5}{8}$  $-\dfrac{1}{6}$ _____

6. $\dfrac{3}{8}$  $-\dfrac{1}{3}$ _____

7. $\dfrac{5}{6}$  $-\dfrac{3}{4}$ _____

8. $\dfrac{7}{8}$  $-\dfrac{1}{3}$ _____

9. $\dfrac{5}{6}$  $-\dfrac{2}{3}$ _____

10. $\dfrac{7}{8}$  $-\dfrac{1}{6}$ _____

11. $\dfrac{3}{8}$  $-\dfrac{1}{6}$ _____

12. $\dfrac{7}{8}$  $-\dfrac{1}{4}$ _____

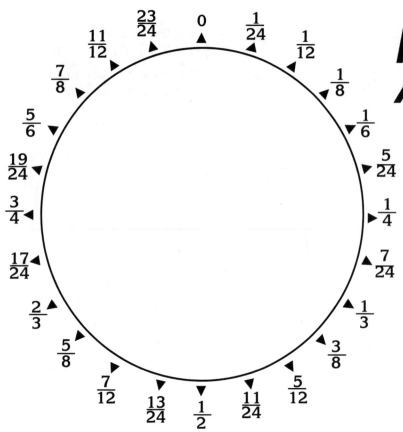

# Fraction Action 66

Please find the differences.
Use sectors to check your answers

1.  $1\dfrac{3}{8}$
    $-\ \dfrac{7}{8}$

2.  $1\dfrac{1}{2}$
    $-\ \dfrac{3}{4}$

3.  $1\dfrac{1}{3}$
    $-\ \dfrac{5}{6}$

4.  $1\dfrac{3}{4}$
    $-\ \dfrac{5}{8}$

5.  $1\dfrac{5}{8}$
    $-\ \dfrac{3}{4}$

6.  $1\dfrac{5}{6}$
    $-\ \dfrac{2}{3}$

7.  $1\dfrac{1}{8}$
    $-\ \dfrac{1}{2}$

8.  $1\dfrac{1}{6}$
    $-\ \dfrac{2}{3}$

9.  $1\dfrac{7}{8}$
    $-1\dfrac{1}{4}$

10. $1\dfrac{1}{4}$
    $-\ \dfrac{5}{8}$

11. $1\dfrac{2}{3}$
    $-\ \dfrac{3}{4}$

12. $1\dfrac{3}{4}$
    $-\ \dfrac{7}{8}$

# Fraction Action 67

Please find the difference in each case. Solve or check, using bars.

Example:

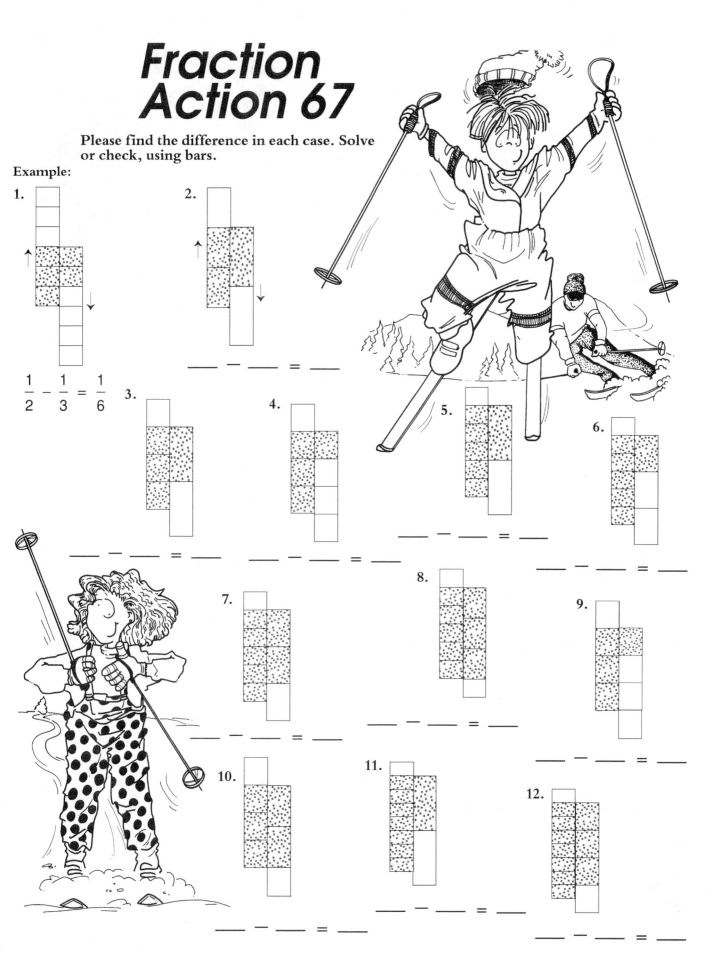

$$\frac{1}{2} - \frac{1}{3} = \frac{1}{6}$$

1.

2.  ___ — ___ = ___

3.  ___ — ___ = ___

4.  ___ — ___ = ___

5.  ___ — ___ = ___

6.  ___ — ___ = ___

7.  ___ — ___ = ___

8.  ___ — ___ = ___

9.  ___ — ___ = ___

10.  ___ — ___ = ___

11.  ___ — ___ = ___

12.  ___ — ___ = ___

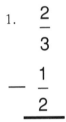

# Fraction Action 68

Please find the differences. Use the fraction ruler to check your answers.

The fraction ruler (left edge):

2

11/12    23/24
5/6      7/8
3/4      19/24
2/3      17/24
7/12     5/8
1/2      13/24
5/12     11/24
1/3      3/8
1/4      7/24
1/6      5/24
1/12     1/8
1        1/24

11/12    23/24
5/6      7/8
3/4      19/24
2/3      17/24
7/12     5/8
1/2      13/24
5/12     11/24
1/3      3/8
1/4      7/24
1/6      5/24
1/12     1/8
         1/24

1.  $\dfrac{2}{3}$
    $-\dfrac{1}{2}$
    ___

2.  $\dfrac{3}{4}$
    $-\dfrac{1}{3}$
    ___

3.  $\dfrac{2}{3}$
    $-\dfrac{1}{4}$
    ___

4.  $\dfrac{3}{4}$
    $-\dfrac{2}{3}$
    ___

5.  $\dfrac{1}{2}$
    $-\dfrac{1}{3}$
    ___

6.  $\dfrac{5}{6}$
    $-\dfrac{1}{4}$
    ___

7.  $\dfrac{5}{6}$
    $-\dfrac{1}{3}$
    ___

8.  $\dfrac{1}{2}$
    $-\dfrac{1}{6}$
    ___

9.  $\dfrac{5}{6}$
    $-\dfrac{2}{3}$
    ___

10. $\dfrac{3}{4}$
    $-\dfrac{1}{6}$
    ___

11. $\dfrac{1}{2}$
    $-\dfrac{1}{4}$
    ___

12. $\dfrac{5}{6}$
    $-\dfrac{3}{4}$
    ___

# Fraction
# Action 69

**Please find the differences. Use the fraction ruler to check your answers.**

Fraction ruler (left margin):

**2**
11/12 · 23/24
5/6 · 7/8
3/4 · 19/24
2/3 · 17/24
7/12 · 5/8
1/2 · 13/24
5/12 · 11/24
1/3 · 3/8
1/4 · 7/24
1/6 · 5/24
1/12 · 1/8
· 1/24

**1**
11/12 · 23/24
5/6 · 7/8
3/4 · 19/24
2/3 · 17/24
7/12 · 5/8
1/2 · 13/24
5/12 · 11/24
1/3 · 3/8
1/4 · 7/24
1/6 · 5/24
1/12 · 1/8
· 1/24

1.  $\dfrac{7}{8}$
  $-\dfrac{1}{2}$

2.  $\dfrac{6}{8}$
  $-\dfrac{1}{4}$

3.  $\dfrac{5}{6}$
  $-\dfrac{1}{4}$

4.  $\dfrac{3}{4}$
  $-\dfrac{2}{3}$

5.  $\dfrac{5}{8}$
  $-\dfrac{1}{6}$

6.  $\dfrac{3}{8}$
  $-\dfrac{1}{3}$

7.  $\dfrac{5}{6}$
  $-\dfrac{3}{4}$

8.  $\dfrac{7}{8}$
  $-\dfrac{1}{3}$

9.  $\dfrac{5}{6}$
  $-\dfrac{2}{3}$

10.  $\dfrac{7}{8}$
  $-\dfrac{1}{6}$

11.  $\dfrac{3}{8}$
  $-\dfrac{1}{6}$

12.  $\dfrac{7}{8}$
  $-\dfrac{1}{4}$

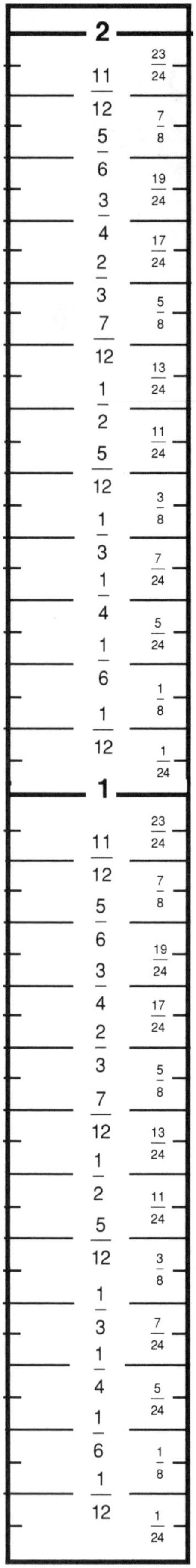
2
23/24
11/12
7/8
5/6
19/24
3/4
17/24
2/3
5/8
7/12
13/24
1/2
11/24
5/12
3/8
1/3
7/24
1/4
5/24
1/6
1/8
1/12
1/24
1
23/24
11/12
7/8
5/6
19/24
3/4
17/24
2/3
5/8
7/12
13/24
1/2
11/24
5/12
3/8
1/3
7/24
1/4
5/24
1/6
1/8
1/12
1/24

# Fraction Action 70

**Please find the differences. Use the fraction ruler to check your answers.**

1. $\frac{1}{2} - \frac{1}{3}$

2. $\frac{3}{4} - \frac{1}{2}$

3. $\frac{3}{8} - \frac{1}{4}$

4. $\frac{7}{8} - \frac{1}{2}$

5. $\frac{5}{8} - \frac{1}{2}$

6. $\frac{1}{2} - \frac{1}{4}$

7. $\frac{1}{3} - \frac{1}{4}$

8. $\frac{7}{8} - \frac{5}{6}$

9. $\frac{3}{4} - \frac{1}{3}$

10. $\frac{7}{8} - \frac{2}{3}$

11. $\frac{5}{6} - \frac{1}{3}$

12. $\frac{2}{3} - \frac{1}{4}$

13. $\frac{5}{8} - \frac{1}{4}$

14. $\frac{3}{8} - \frac{1}{3}$

15. $\frac{7}{8} - \frac{3}{4}$

| | |
|---|---|
| $\frac{11}{12}$ | $\frac{23}{24}$ |
| $\frac{5}{6}$ | $\frac{7}{8}$ |
| $\frac{3}{4}$ | $\frac{19}{24}$ |
| $\frac{2}{3}$ | $\frac{17}{24}$ |
| $\frac{7}{12}$ | $\frac{5}{8}$ |
| $\frac{1}{2}$ | $\frac{13}{24}$ |
| $\frac{5}{12}$ | $\frac{11}{24}$ |
| $\frac{1}{3}$ | $\frac{3}{8}$ |
| $\frac{1}{4}$ | $\frac{7}{24}$ |
| $\frac{1}{6}$ | $\frac{5}{24}$ |
| $\frac{1}{12}$ | $\frac{1}{8}$ |
| | $\frac{1}{24}$ |
| **1** | |
| $\frac{11}{12}$ | $\frac{23}{24}$ |
| $\frac{5}{6}$ | $\frac{7}{8}$ |
| $\frac{3}{4}$ | $\frac{19}{24}$ |
| $\frac{2}{3}$ | $\frac{17}{24}$ |
| $\frac{7}{12}$ | $\frac{5}{8}$ |
| $\frac{1}{2}$ | $\frac{13}{24}$ |
| $\frac{5}{12}$ | $\frac{11}{24}$ |
| $\frac{1}{3}$ | $\frac{3}{8}$ |
| $\frac{1}{4}$ | $\frac{7}{24}$ |
| $\frac{1}{6}$ | $\frac{5}{24}$ |
| $\frac{1}{12}$ | $\frac{1}{8}$ |
| | $\frac{1}{24}$ |

# Fraction Action 71

**Please find the differences. Use the fraction ruler to check your answers.**

1. $1\frac{3}{8}$
$-\ \frac{7}{8}$

2. $1\frac{1}{2}$
$-\ \frac{3}{4}$

3. $1\frac{1}{3}$
$-\ \frac{5}{6}$

4. $1\frac{3}{4}$
$-\ \frac{5}{8}$

5. $1\frac{5}{8}$
$-\ \frac{3}{4}$

6. $1\frac{5}{6}$
$-\ \frac{2}{3}$

7. $1\frac{1}{8}$
$-\ \frac{1}{2}$

8. $1\frac{1}{6}$
$-\ \frac{2}{3}$

9. $1\frac{7}{8}$
$-1\frac{1}{4}$

10. $1\frac{1}{4}$
$-\ \frac{5}{8}$

11. $1\frac{2}{3}$
$-\ \frac{3}{4}$

12. $1\frac{3}{4}$
$-\ \frac{7}{8}$

# Fractions in the Pie Shop

An analysis of the standard algorithm for subtracting mixed numbers reveals why it makes little sense to most students. It is unnecessarily complex. Fortunately, an easier and more sensible algorithm exists.

A step by step look at the standard algorithm is instructive. Consider the problem: $4\frac{1}{4} - 1\frac{1}{2}$

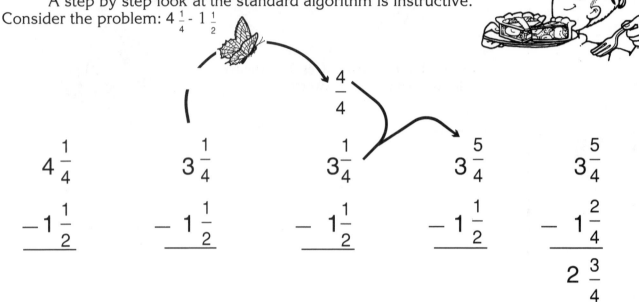

$$4\frac{1}{4}$$
$$-1\frac{1}{2}$$

$$3\frac{1}{4}$$
$$-1\frac{1}{2}$$

$$3\frac{1}{4}$$
$$-1\frac{1}{2}$$

$$3\frac{5}{4}$$
$$-1\frac{1}{2}$$

$$3\frac{5}{4}$$
$$-1\frac{2}{4}$$
$$2\frac{3}{4}$$

In the standard algorithm, the fraction is subtracted from the fraction and the whole number from the whole number. Since $\frac{1}{2}$ is greater than $\frac{1}{4}$, it is necessary in this instance to regroup, borrowing from the whole number. One is borrowed from 4 leaving 3. The 1 undergoes a metamorphosis by which it is transformed into $\frac{4}{4}$. The $\frac{4}{4}$ lands on the $\frac{1}{4}$ and the two merge to make $\frac{5}{4}$. Next the $\frac{1}{2}$ is replaced by its equivalent $\frac{2}{4}$. Then the 1 is subtracted from the 3 and the $\frac{2}{4}$ from the $\frac{5}{4}$ leaving $2\frac{3}{4}$. In this five-step process, two steps take place mentally, a process that is too abstract for some students. This is a textbook rather than a real-world algorithm.

Compare this with the procedure often used in the real world. For this a visit to a pie shop is instructive. The pie shop owner is very neat and always uses the fewest possible plates. Being very consumer oriented, the owner tries to be as flexible as necessary to assure customer satisfaction. On this occasion, there are $4\frac{1}{4}$ apple pies remaining to be sold. (The shaded part indicates empty pie plate areas.)

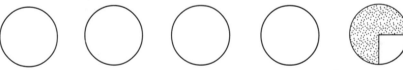

A customer comes in and asks to purchase $1\frac{1}{2}$ apple pies. The owner boxes up a whole pie and then cuts one of the remaining *whole* pies in half. The half pie is boxed up and the customer's order is completed for $1\frac{1}{2}$ pies with a smile.

After the customer leaves there are two whole pies, a half pie, and a quarter pie remaining.

The shelf is tidied by putting the half and quarter pie into the same plate and removing the empty plate. The owner notes that the two pieces total three-quarters of a pie, realizing that there are $2\frac{3}{4}$ pies remaining to be sold.

How does this pie shop, real-life mathematics translate into an algorithm?

$$4\frac{1}{4} \qquad \quad 4 \qquad \frac{1}{4} \qquad\qquad 4 \qquad \frac{1}{4}$$
$$-1\frac{1}{2} \qquad -1\frac{1}{2} \qquad\qquad -1\frac{1}{2}$$
$$\overline{\phantom{4\frac{1}{4}}} \qquad \overline{\phantom{4\frac{1}{4}}} \qquad\qquad \overline{\phantom{4\frac{1}{4}}}$$
$$2\frac{1}{2} + \frac{1}{4} \qquad\qquad 2\frac{2}{4} + \frac{1}{4} = 2\frac{3}{4}$$

The pie shop algorithm simplifies the process in several ways and plays to student strength in addition. In contrast to the standard algorithm, the mixed number in the subtrahend is subtracted from the whole number in the minuend. Nothing is ever subtracted from the fraction in the minuend. It is put aside temporarily.

The student can think this way: From $1\frac{1}{2}$ to 2 is a trip of $\frac{1}{2}$ unit. From 2 to 4 is a trip of 2 units. From 4 to $4\frac{1}{4}$ is a trip of $\frac{1}{4}$ unit. The three trips together total $2\frac{3}{4}$. This is an additive approach with which students are already familiar at this stage.

The advantages are that the mental metamorphosis step is eliminated, the final process is one of addition rather than subtraction, all steps in the algorithm are visible, and there are fewer steps. Most students quickly realize that this new algorithm is real world-like which gives it meaning in sharp contrast to the standard algorithm.

This approach has been used successfully with students who have had great difficulty with fractions and those with learning disabilities. The following steps are recommended:

1. Begin using only pie models and oral communication.
2. Pose problems such as the example above in which the difference between two mixed numbers is to be determined. First, use mixed numbers with like denominators where borrowing is not required, then mixed numbers with like denominators where borrowing is required, and finally mixed numbers with unlike denominators where borrowing is required.
3. After the students understand the process in the pie shop, make a step by step record that relates each notation with an action with the manipulatives. Students should leave this activity with a manipulative and mental picture of what is happening in the process. They will find the process to be meaningful because of its real-world parallel.

Fraction Action 72 is designed to be used as a follow-up to the instruction experiences described. The pie shop scenario is maintained to help students recollect their previous experience. The sheet of pie cutouts is sufficient for two students. Mount on card stock and have students cut out whole pies and the pie pieces. The empty plates (those that are shaded) are for placing the pieces into one plate after each sale. Correct records will look like this:

A. $4\frac{1}{4} - 1\frac{3}{4} = 2\frac{1}{2}$

B. $4\frac{1}{3} - 1\frac{2}{3} = 2\frac{2}{3}$

C. $3\frac{1}{4} - 1\frac{1}{2} = 1\frac{3}{4}$

D. $3\frac{1}{2} - 1\frac{3}{4} = 1\frac{3}{4}$

E. $3\frac{1}{6} - 1\frac{2}{3} = 1\frac{1}{2}$

F. $4\frac{1}{3} - 2\frac{2}{3} = 1\frac{2}{3}$

# Pie Shop Circles

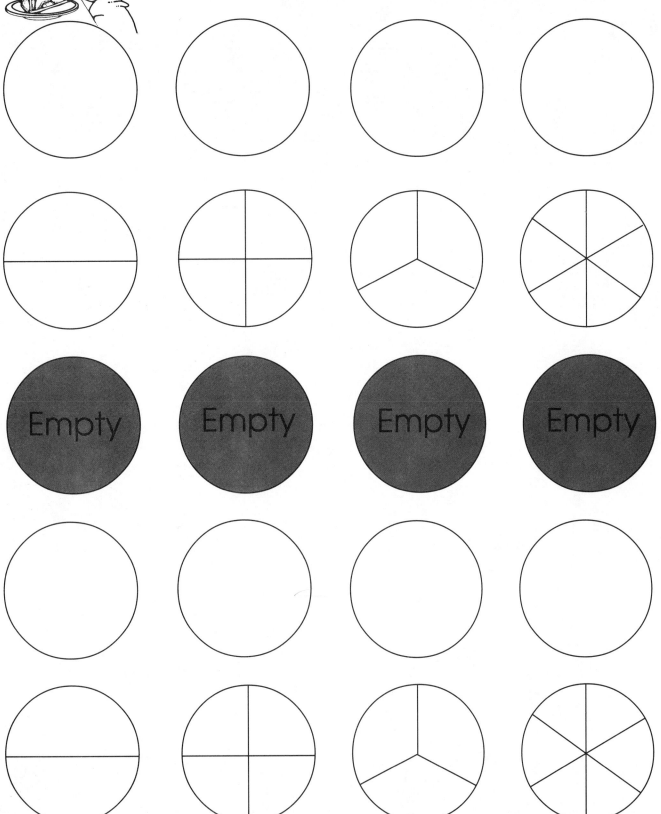

# Fraction Action 72

You are the pie shop owner. In each case, the pies for sale are shown. The shaded parts indicate empty pie plate areas. Please use paper pies and pie pieces to show the sale in transaction. After each sale, tidy up by placing remaining pieces into a single plate so the fewest number of plates are used. Make a pictorial record of how the pies look after all this and a written record of the total transaction.

| | Pies for Sale | Purchase | Pies for Sale | Record |
|---|---|---|---|---|
| A | | $1\frac{3}{4}$ | | |
| B | | $1\frac{2}{3}$ | | |
| C | | $1\frac{1}{2}$ | | |
| D | | $1\frac{3}{4}$ | | |
| E | | $1\frac{2}{3}$ | | |
| F | | $2\frac{2}{3}$ | | |

# Part 5

## Addition and Subtraction of Fractions using Egg Carton Method

Egg cartons provide concrete experiences that assist in building an understanding of important fraction concepts such as representing, adding, and subtracting fractions. The 12 cavities facilitate the division of the carton into halves, thirds, fourths, sixths, and twelfths. This family includes those fractions that are involved in a high percentage of real-life applications.

Meaning is developed at the concrete, pictorial, and symbolic levels. This reflects the Piagetian progression of learning. By continuously moving among these forms, students gain an understanding of their interrelatedness. Each level makes its unique contribution to the construction of meaning. Multiple representations are recommended in all of the reform documents. The natural progression from the concrete to understanding leads to the effective development of a rich spectrum of meaning.

The experiences can be traced in the *AIMS Model of Mathematics*. The concrete activities correspond to the circle, the pictorial to the square, the symbolic to the triangle, and the development of understanding to the hexagon (see page iii).

Egg cartons are a part of most every child's world. By building an association between egg cartons and the fraction concepts treated in this section, students will have a frequent reminder of the role 12 and its factors play in the use of fractions in addition and subtraction.

The required concrete materials are readily available and inexpensive. Each student needs two egg cartons and markers such as beans, small pebbles, chips, or other uniform objects. Drawings of egg cartons are included in the *Appendix* for making copies in the event egg cartons are not available. Wherever possible, however, it is suggested that actual egg cartons be used.

*Fraction Action 73* deals with denominators exclusively. The cartons are to be divided into equal parts or fair shares using cords or strips of paper. All except *E* can be done in more than one way. Understanding is enriched by the discovery of more than one way to form equal parts. Students are to be encouraged to share the ways in which they have divided the carton into halves, thirds, fourths, and sixths.

*Fraction Action 74* asks students to represent fractions by representing both numerators and denominators. The denominator sections the carton (as in activity 73) and the numerator is represented by filling the cavities in an appropriate number of those sections.

In *Fraction Action 75 – 77,* addition is introduced using the manipulative, representational, and abstract approaches. The addend fractions are formed and added by combining objects into one carton or filling one carton and leaving the remainder in a second if the sum is greater than one.

Subtraction activities are found in *Fraction Action 78 – 81*. The difference with addition quickly becomes obvious. Whereas there are two addends in addition, in subtraction the process begins with the whole and it is broken into two parts: the part subtracted and the part remaining after subtraction. In other words, the minuend is divided into two addends.

# Fraction
# Action 73

Using cords or strips of paper, please divide the egg carton into the number of equal parts requested. Try doing it in more than one way. Please illustrate your solutions in the pictures below. Name the kind of parts that are formed.

A.  Egg carton divided into two equal parts          Name of parts:

B.  Egg carton divided into three equal parts          Name of parts:

C.  Egg carton divided into four equal parts          Name of parts:

D.  Egg carton divided into six equal parts          Name of parts:

E.  Egg carton divided into twelve equal parts          Name of parts:

# Fraction
# Action 74

Using cords or strips of paper, please divide the egg carton into the proper number of equal regions. Place objects into cavities of the egg carton to picture the fraction named.

A. $\frac{1}{4}$ or one-fourth:

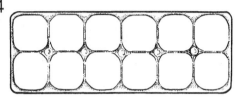

B. $\frac{3}{4}$ or three-fourths:

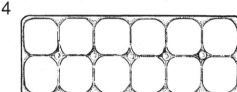

C. $\frac{1}{3}$ or one-third:

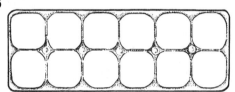

D. $\frac{1}{2}$ or one-half:

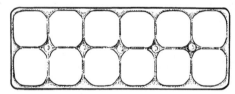

E. $\frac{2}{3}$ or two-thirds:

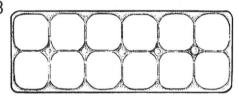

F. $\frac{2}{4}$ or two-fourths:

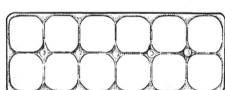

G. $\frac{1}{6}$ or one-sixth:

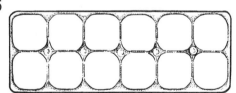

H. $\frac{5}{6}$ or five-sixths:

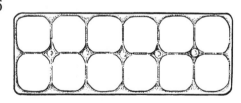

H. $\frac{5}{12}$ or five-twelfths:

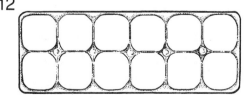

I. $\frac{5}{7}$ or seven-twelfths:

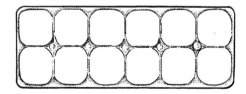

# Fraction
# Action 75

Please build models of the fractions in separate cartons. Add by moving objects into the "After" carton. Draw a picture of the result. Complete the sentence showing the addends and sum.

1. $\dfrac{1}{2} + \dfrac{1}{3} =$

2. $\dfrac{1}{3} + \dfrac{1}{6} =$

3. $\dfrac{1}{4} + \dfrac{1}{2} =$

4. $\dfrac{1}{4} + \dfrac{1}{3} =$

5. $\dfrac{2}{3} + \dfrac{1}{6} =$

6. $\dfrac{3}{4} + \dfrac{1}{6} =$

7. $\dfrac{5}{6} + \dfrac{1}{12} =$

8. $\dfrac{1}{2} + \dfrac{1}{6} =$

9. $\dfrac{7}{12} + \dfrac{1}{4} =$

10. $\dfrac{3}{4} + \dfrac{1}{12} =$

# Fraction
# Action 76

Please build models of the fractions in separate cartons. Add by moving objects ito the "After" cartons, filling one first before placing objects in the second. Draw a picture of the result. Complete the sentence showing the addends and sum.

|  | Before | After |  | Before | After |
|---|---|---|---|---|---|
| 1. | $\frac{3}{4} + \frac{2}{3} =$ | | 2. | $\frac{1}{2} + \frac{5}{6} =$ | |
| 3. | $\frac{2}{3} + \frac{5}{6} =$ | | 4. | $\frac{1}{4} + \frac{5}{6} =$ | |
| 5. | $\frac{1}{2} + \frac{2}{3} =$ | | 6. | $\frac{3}{4} + \frac{1}{2} =$ | |
| 7. | $\frac{3}{4} + \frac{7}{12} =$ | | 8. | $\frac{1}{3} + \frac{3}{4} =$ | |
| 9. | $\frac{5}{6} + \frac{3}{4} =$ | | 10. | $\frac{5}{6} + \frac{1}{3} =$ | |

# Fraction
# Action 77

Please build models of the fractions in separate cartons. Add by moving objects into the "After" cartons, filling one first before placing objects in the second. Draw a picture of the result. Complete the sentence showing the addends and sum.

Before    After

1. $\dfrac{1}{2} + \dfrac{5}{12} =$

2. $\dfrac{3}{4} + \dfrac{5}{12} =$

3. $\dfrac{7}{12} + \dfrac{5}{6} =$

4. $\dfrac{4}{12} + \dfrac{3}{4} =$

5. $\dfrac{2}{3} + \dfrac{2}{3} =$

6. $\dfrac{5}{12} + \dfrac{2}{3} =$

7. $\dfrac{5}{6} + \dfrac{5}{6} =$

8. $\dfrac{1}{2} + \dfrac{7}{12} =$

9. $\dfrac{3}{4} + \dfrac{3}{4} =$

10. $\dfrac{11}{12} + \dfrac{1}{2} =$

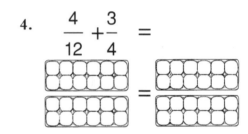

# Fraction
# Action 78

Please build a model of the minuend. Subtract the amount indicated by removing it from the egg carton. Draw a before and after picture. Complete the subtraction sentence by writing in the difference.

1. **Before**        **After**

$$\frac{1}{2} - \frac{1}{3} =$$

⬚⬚⬚⬚⬚⬚ $- \frac{1}{3} =$ ⬚⬚⬚⬚⬚⬚

2. **Before**        **After**

$$\frac{2}{3} - \frac{1}{4} =$$

⬚⬚⬚⬚⬚⬚ $- \frac{1}{4} =$ ⬚⬚⬚⬚⬚⬚

3. $$\frac{3}{4} - \frac{1}{3} =$$

⬚⬚⬚⬚⬚⬚ $- \frac{1}{3} =$ ⬚⬚⬚⬚⬚⬚

4. $$\frac{5}{6} - \frac{3}{4} =$$

⬚⬚⬚⬚⬚⬚ $- \frac{3}{4} =$ ⬚⬚⬚⬚⬚⬚

5. $$\frac{1}{3} - \frac{1}{4} =$$

⬚⬚⬚⬚⬚⬚ $- \frac{1}{4} =$ ⬚⬚⬚⬚⬚⬚

6. $$\frac{5}{6} - \frac{2}{3} =$$

⬚⬚⬚⬚⬚⬚ $- \frac{2}{3} =$ ⬚⬚⬚⬚⬚⬚

7. $$\frac{1}{2} - \frac{1}{4} =$$

⬚⬚⬚⬚⬚⬚ $- \frac{1}{4} =$ ⬚⬚⬚⬚⬚⬚

8. $$\frac{1}{4} - \frac{1}{6} =$$

⬚⬚⬚⬚⬚⬚ $- \frac{1}{6} =$ ⬚⬚⬚⬚⬚⬚

9. $$\frac{5}{6} - \frac{1}{3} =$$

⬚⬚⬚⬚⬚⬚ $- \frac{1}{3} =$ ⬚⬚⬚⬚⬚⬚

10. $$\frac{2}{3} - \frac{1}{2} =$$

⬚⬚⬚⬚⬚⬚ $- \frac{1}{2} =$ ⬚⬚⬚⬚⬚⬚

# Fraction Action 79

Please build a model of the minuend. Subtract the amount indicated by removing it from the egg carton. Draw a before and after picture. Complete the subtraction sentence by writing in the difference.

1.  **Before**                    **After**

$$\frac{1}{2} - \frac{1}{6} =$$

⬚⬚⬚⬚⬚⬚ $- \frac{1}{6} =$ ⬚⬚⬚⬚⬚⬚

2.  **Before**                    **After**

$$\frac{5}{6} - \frac{1}{4} =$$

⬚⬚⬚⬚⬚⬚ $- \frac{1}{4} =$ ⬚⬚⬚⬚⬚⬚

3.  $$\frac{3}{4} - \frac{1}{2} =$$

⬚⬚⬚⬚⬚⬚ $- \frac{1}{2} =$ ⬚⬚⬚⬚⬚⬚

4.  $$\frac{1}{3} - \frac{1}{6} =$$

⬚⬚⬚⬚⬚⬚ $- \frac{1}{6} =$ ⬚⬚⬚⬚⬚⬚

5.  $$\frac{2}{3} - \frac{1}{6} =$$

⬚⬚⬚⬚⬚⬚ $- \frac{1}{6} =$ ⬚⬚⬚⬚⬚⬚

6.  $$\frac{3}{4} - \frac{1}{4} =$$

⬚⬚⬚⬚⬚⬚ $- \frac{1}{4} =$ ⬚⬚⬚⬚⬚⬚

7.  $$\frac{5}{6} - \frac{1}{2} =$$

⬚⬚⬚⬚⬚⬚ $- \frac{1}{2} =$ ⬚⬚⬚⬚⬚⬚

8.  $$\frac{3}{4} - \frac{2}{3} =$$

⬚⬚⬚⬚⬚⬚ $- \frac{2}{3} =$ ⬚⬚⬚⬚⬚⬚

9.  $$\frac{3}{4} - \frac{1}{6} =$$

⬚⬚⬚⬚⬚⬚ $- \frac{1}{6} =$ ⬚⬚⬚⬚⬚⬚

10.  $$\frac{1}{3} - \frac{1}{12} =$$

⬚⬚⬚⬚⬚⬚ $- \frac{1}{12} =$ ⬚⬚⬚⬚⬚⬚

# Fraction
# Action 80

Please build a model of the minuend. Subtract the amount indicated by removing it from the egg carton. Draw a before and after picture. Complete the subtraction sentence by writing in the difference.

| Before | After | | Before | After |
|---|---|---|---|---|

1.  $1\frac{1}{2} - \frac{3}{4} =$

 $- \frac{3}{4} =$

2.  $1\frac{1}{3} - \frac{5}{6} =$

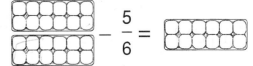 $- \frac{5}{6} =$

3.  $1\frac{2}{3} - \frac{3}{4} =$

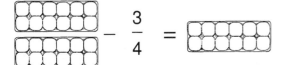 $- \frac{3}{4} =$

4.  $1\frac{1}{4} - \frac{1}{2} =$

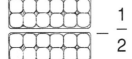 $- \frac{1}{2} =$

5.  $1\frac{1}{6} - \frac{3}{4} =$

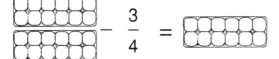 $- \frac{3}{4} =$

6.  $1\frac{1}{2} - \frac{5}{6} =$

 $- \frac{5}{6} =$

7.  $1\frac{3}{4} - \frac{5}{6} =$

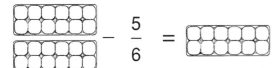 $- \frac{5}{6} =$

8.  $1\frac{1}{4} - \frac{3}{4} =$

 $- \frac{3}{4} =$

9.  $1\frac{1}{2} - \frac{2}{3} =$

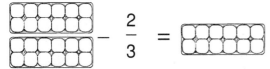 $- \frac{2}{3} =$

10.  $1\frac{1}{3} - \frac{3}{4} =$

 $- \frac{3}{4} =$

# Fraction Action 81

**Please build a model of the minuend. Subtract the amount indicated by removing it from the egg carton. Draw a before and after picture. Complete the subtraction sentence by writing in the difference.**

|  | Before | After |  | Before | After |

1. $1\dfrac{1}{2} - \dfrac{7}{12} =$

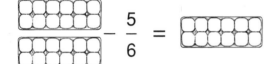

2. $1\dfrac{1}{3} - \dfrac{1}{2} =$

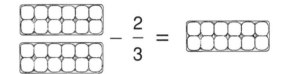

3. $1\dfrac{2}{3} - \dfrac{5}{6} =$

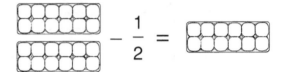

4. $1\dfrac{1}{4} - \dfrac{2}{3} =$

5. $1\dfrac{1}{6} - \dfrac{1}{2} =$

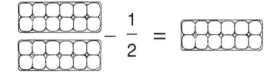

6. $1\dfrac{1}{3} - \dfrac{2}{3} =$

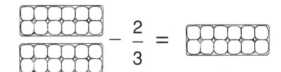

7. $1\dfrac{1}{4} - \dfrac{5}{6} =$

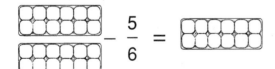

8. $1\dfrac{1}{4} - \dfrac{5}{12} =$

9. $1\dfrac{1}{3} - \dfrac{7}{12} =$

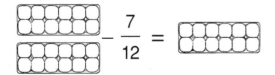

10. $1\dfrac{1}{6} - \dfrac{2}{3} =$

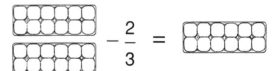

# Multiplication of Fractions

### Part 6

In mathematics, multiplication is generally represented by two mutually perpendicular measures whose product is a measure of area. For example, the length and width of a rectangle are mutually perpendicular and their product is a measure of the area of the rectangle.

Width = 2

Length = 3

Area = 6

In the unit square model, this same perpendicular relationship exists. To represent the denominator of the first factor, lines are drawn parallel to one side to create the number of congruent subdivisions named by its denominator. The numerator is represented by shading in the number of these spaces it names.

To multiply by the second factor, the same procedure is followed except that the dividing lines are drawn perpendicular to those in the first instance.

thirds

$\frac{1}{3}$

The total number of subdivisions formed represents the denominator of the product. The number of subdivisions in which the numerators overlap names the numerator of the product.

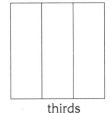  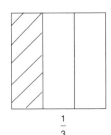 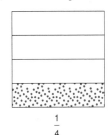 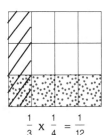

thirds        fourths              $\frac{1}{3}$              $\frac{1}{4}$              $\frac{1}{3}$ x $\frac{1}{4}$ = $\frac{1}{12}$

Included with this publication is a set of AIMS Fraction Squares that help model the multiplication of fractions. The set consists of transparent unit squares that show the fractions $\frac{1}{2}, \frac{1}{3}, \frac{2}{3}, \frac{1}{4}, \frac{3}{4}, \frac{2}{5}, \frac{3}{5}, \frac{1}{6}$, and $\frac{5}{6}$. The multiplication of two fractions is modeled by superimposing the model of one fraction on top of the model of a second fraction with dividing lines running perpendicular to the first. This set is excellent for overhead use in conjunction with any activity in this part.

To meet the specific needs of students, teachers may wish to reorder the sequence in which these activities are used.

In *Fraction Action 82 – 84,* students are asked to draw pictures of the two fraction factors. Reference to the AIMS Fraction Squares is particularly effective at this stage. The product is read from the completed picture and recorded to complete the sentence.

*Fraction Action 85* and *86* require reading the pictures to determine the factors and the products. *Fraction Action 87* has students identify the factors and product, find, and complete the matching sentence. This activity works will as an assessment.

The use of the distributive property in the multiplication of mixed numbers is addressed in *Fraction Action 88* and *89.*

An alternative algorithm for the division of fractions is introduced for use with *Fraction Action 90.* This method is more consistent with the mathematical nature of the process of division, particularly as it relates to it as the inverse of multiplication.

a. Please represent the problem
   graphically.
b. Determine the product from the
   drawing and complete the sentence.

# Fraction Action 82

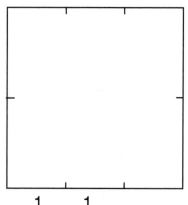

$$\frac{1}{2} \times \frac{1}{3} =$$

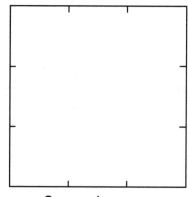

$$\frac{2}{3} \times \frac{1}{3} =$$

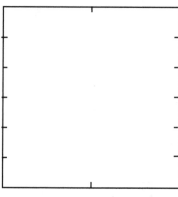

$$\frac{1}{6} \times \frac{1}{2} =$$

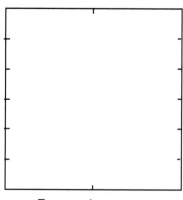

$$\frac{2}{3} \times \frac{1}{2} =$$

$$\frac{5}{6} \times \frac{1}{2} =$$

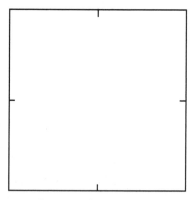

$$\frac{1}{2} \times \frac{1}{2} =$$

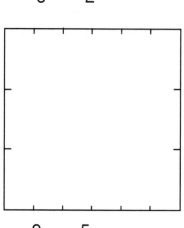

$$\frac{1}{3} \times \frac{1}{3} =$$

$$\frac{2}{3} \times \frac{5}{6} =$$

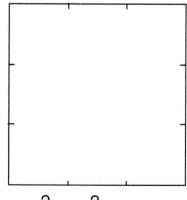

$$\frac{2}{3} \times \frac{2}{3} =$$

a. Please find the following products.
b. Check your result using the AIMS Fraction Squares.

# Fraction Action 82
## – part 2

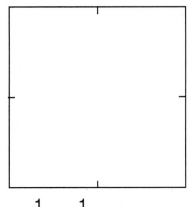

$$\frac{1}{2} \times \frac{1}{2} =$$

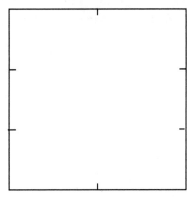

$$\frac{2}{3} \times \frac{1}{2} =$$

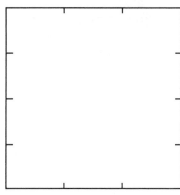

$$\frac{3}{4} \times \frac{1}{3} =$$

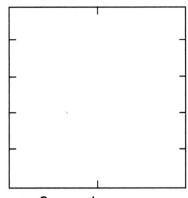

$$\frac{2}{5} \times \frac{1}{2} =$$

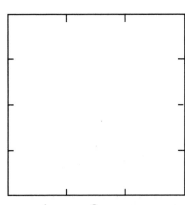

$$\frac{1}{4} \times \frac{2}{3} =$$

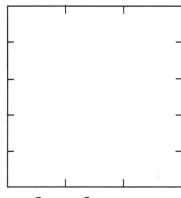

$$\frac{3}{5} \times \frac{2}{3} =$$

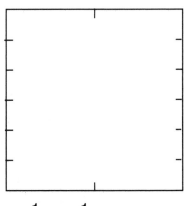

$$\frac{1}{6} \times \frac{1}{2} =$$

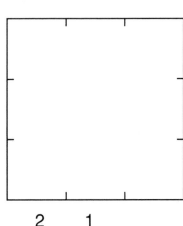

$$\frac{2}{3} \times \frac{1}{3}$$

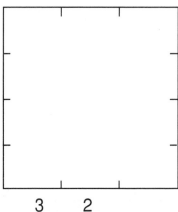

$$\frac{3}{4} \times \frac{2}{3} =$$

93

# Fraction Action 83

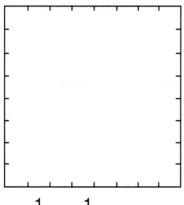

$$\frac{1}{2} \times \frac{1}{4} =$$

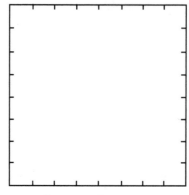

$$\frac{3}{4} \times \frac{3}{4} =$$

$$\frac{1}{2} \times \frac{3}{8} =$$

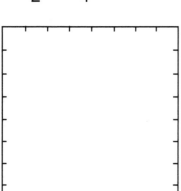

$$\frac{1}{4} \times \frac{3}{4} =$$

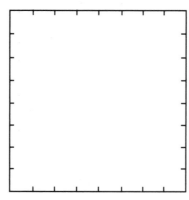

$$\frac{3}{4} \times \frac{1}{2} =$$

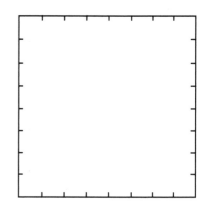

$$\frac{1}{4} \times \frac{1}{4} =$$

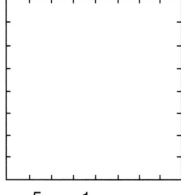

$$\frac{5}{8} \times \frac{1}{2} =$$

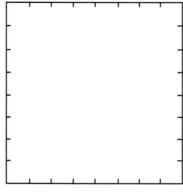

$$\frac{3}{4} \times \frac{3}{4} =$$

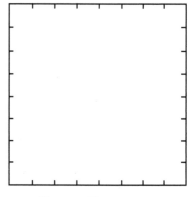

$$\frac{7}{8} \times \frac{3}{4} =$$

94

# Fraction
# Action 83 – *part 2*

Use your AIMS Fraction Squares to find the folowing products.

1. $\dfrac{1}{2} \times \dfrac{2}{5} =$

2. $\dfrac{1}{6} \times \dfrac{2}{3} =$

3. $\dfrac{1}{4} \times \dfrac{1}{4} =$

4. $\dfrac{3}{4} \times \dfrac{5}{6} =$

5. $\dfrac{3}{5} \times \dfrac{1}{2} =$

6. $\dfrac{1}{3} \times \dfrac{5}{6} =$

7. $\dfrac{2}{3} \times \dfrac{2}{3} =$

8. $\dfrac{2}{5} \times \dfrac{3}{5} =$

9. $\dfrac{1}{2} \times \dfrac{5}{6} =$

10. $\dfrac{1}{6} \times \dfrac{1}{3} =$

11. $\dfrac{2}{5} \times \dfrac{2}{3} =$

12. $\dfrac{5}{6} \times \dfrac{5}{6} =$

13. $\dfrac{3}{5} \times \dfrac{5}{6} =$

14. $\dfrac{1}{4} \times \dfrac{1}{6} =$

a. **Please represent the problem graphically.**
b. **Determine the product from the drawing and complete the sentence.**

# Fraction Action 84

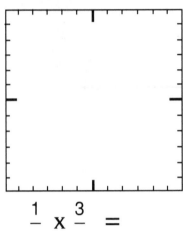

$$\frac{1}{3} \times \frac{3}{4} =$$

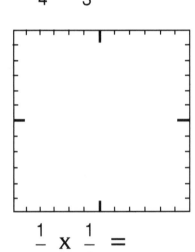

$$\frac{1}{4} \times \frac{2}{3} =$$

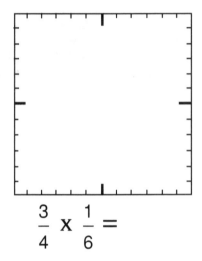

$$\frac{3}{4} \times \frac{1}{6} =$$

$$\frac{1}{4} \times \frac{5}{6} =$$

$$\frac{1}{4} \times \frac{1}{3} =$$

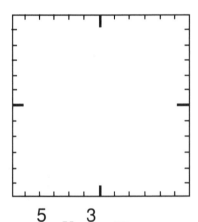

$$\frac{5}{6} \times \frac{3}{4} =$$

$$\frac{2}{3} \times \frac{3}{4} =$$

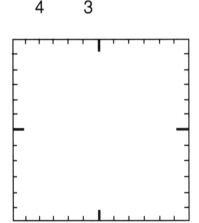

$$\frac{1}{4} \times \frac{1}{6} =$$

$$\frac{3}{4} \times \frac{5}{12} =$$

# Fraction
# Action 84 – *part 2*

Use your AIMS Fraction Squares to find the folowing products.

1. $\dfrac{1}{3} \times \dfrac{1}{3} =$

2. $\dfrac{1}{4} \times \dfrac{5}{6} =$

3. $\dfrac{3}{4} \times \dfrac{3}{5} =$

4. $\dfrac{2}{5} \times \dfrac{5}{6} =$

5. $\dfrac{1}{2} \times \dfrac{1}{3} =$

6. $\dfrac{1}{4} \times \dfrac{1}{3} =$

7. $\dfrac{3}{5} \times \dfrac{1}{4} =$

8. $\dfrac{2}{3} \times \dfrac{1}{6} =$

9. $\dfrac{1}{3} \times \dfrac{1}{4} =$

10. $\dfrac{3}{4} \times \dfrac{1}{2} =$

11. $\dfrac{3}{5} \times \dfrac{1}{3} =$

12. $\dfrac{2}{3} \times \dfrac{5}{6} =$

13. $\dfrac{1}{6} \times \dfrac{3}{4} =$

14. $\dfrac{3}{5} \times \dfrac{2}{5} =$

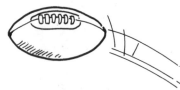

# Fraction
# Action 85

Determine the factors and products in the pictures.
Write the number sentence that describes each.

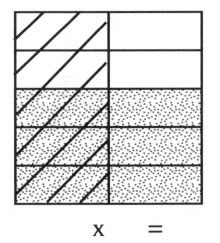

X ___ = ___

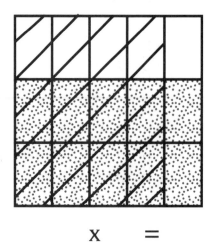

X ___ = ___

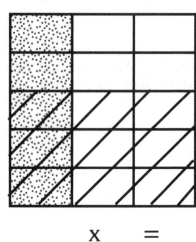

X ___ = ___

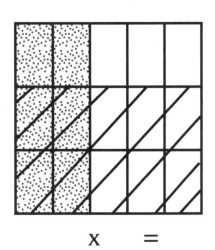

X ___ = ___

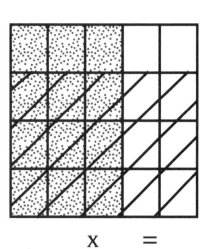

X ___ = ___

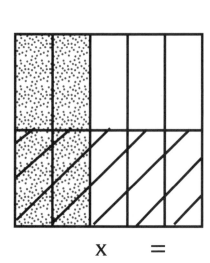

X ___ = ___

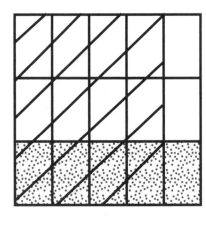

X ___ = ___

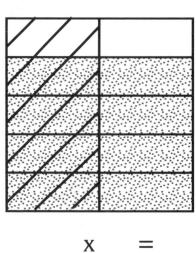

X ___ = ___

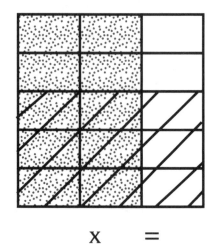

X ___ = ___

# Fraction
# Action 86

Determine the factors and products in the pictures.
Write the number sentence that describes each.

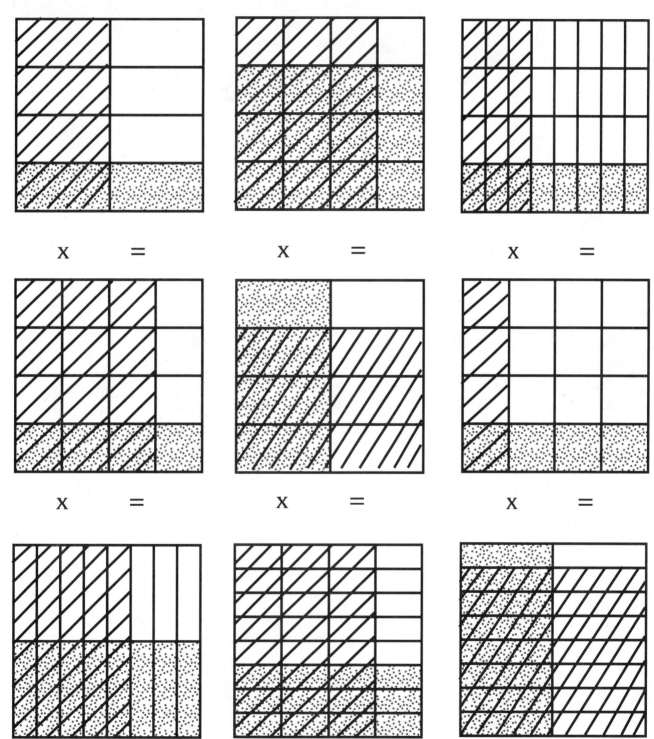

X _____ = _____    X _____ = _____    X _____ = _____

X _____ = _____    X _____ = _____    X _____ = _____

X _____ = _____    X _____ = _____    X _____ = _____

# Fraction Action 87

**Please match each picture to a sentence below.
Then complete the sentence by writing the answer.**

_____ 1. $\dfrac{1}{3} \times \dfrac{1}{3} =$ _____

_____ 2. $\dfrac{3}{4} \times \dfrac{2}{3} =$ _____

_____ 3. $\dfrac{1}{3} \times \dfrac{1}{2} =$ _____

_____ 4. $\dfrac{3}{5} \times \dfrac{2}{3} =$ _____

_____ 5. $\dfrac{1}{2} \times \dfrac{2}{5} =$ _____

_____ 6. $\dfrac{2}{3} \times \dfrac{1}{4} =$ _____

_____ 7. $\dfrac{1}{2} \times \dfrac{1}{2} =$ _____

_____ 8. $\dfrac{1}{3} \times \dfrac{3}{4} =$ _____

_____ 9. $\dfrac{1}{4} \times \dfrac{1}{2} =$ _____

_____ 10. $\dfrac{2}{3} \times \dfrac{1}{3} =$ _____

_____ 11. $\dfrac{3}{4} \times \dfrac{3}{4} =$ _____

_____ 12. $\dfrac{3}{5} \times \dfrac{1}{2} =$ _____

_____ 13. $\dfrac{2}{3} \times \dfrac{1}{2} =$ _____

_____ 14. $\dfrac{1}{2} \times \dfrac{1}{6} =$ _____

_____ 15. $\dfrac{1}{2} \times \dfrac{3}{4} =$ _____

_____ 16. $\dfrac{1}{4} \times \dfrac{3}{4} =$ _____

# The Distributive Property
## and the Multiplication of Mixed Numbers

The distributive property of multiplication over addition underlies all multiplication operations in arithmetic and algebra. Yet, the standard multiplication algorithm used in arithmetic masks the distributive property, hides the "ten-ness" of our numeration system, and is not transferable into algebra. It appears to be an efficient "bag of tricks" that somehow leads to the right answer.

The standard algorithm for the multiplication of mixed numbers suffers from similar deficiencies. Is there a better alternative?

The answer is yes! It lies in using the algebraic approach to the distributive property of multiplication over addition. Does this alternative apply to mixed numbers as well as whole numbers and decimals? Again, the answer is yes.

Algebraically, the product of x + y and 2x is found as shown below:

$$2x\,(x + y) = 2x^2 + 2xy$$

The product of two binomials is found as follows:

$$(x + y)(2x + 3y) = 2x^2 + 3xy + 2xy + 3y^2$$

With whole numbers, this gives rise to two algorithms, the *algebraic form* and *display multiplication*. Consider the problem 47 x 89.

Algebraic form: $(40 + 7)(80 + 9) = 3200 + 360 + 560 + 63 = 4183$

Display method:

```
          89
         x47
          63    (7 x 9)
         560    (7 x 80)
         360    (40 x 9)
        3200    (40 x 80)
        4183
```

Both make an important contribution to understanding in that they bring out the "ten-ness" of our numeration system. In the algebraic form units, tens, hundreds, etc., are separated. The display method requires constant attention to place value, thus emphasizing the ten-ness of the numeration system.

It is interesting to note that both methods yield the same sub-products albeit in reverse order. Each is straightforward, devoid of shortcuts that involve meaningless procedures.

A companion element consistent with these algorithms is found in the graphical representation of multiplication shown below. These pictures are powerful for clarifying concepts and processes and reinforcing meaning. Modeling the multiplication of multi-digit numbers and fractions consists of

    1. representing addends within factors as line segments laid end to end,

    2. representing multiplication as a perpendicular array of the factors, specifically as the dimensions of a rectangle, and

    3. completing the rectangle, whose area represents the product.

This illustration is similar to that found in many algebra texts. It pictures $(x + y)(x + y)$.

| $y$ | $xy$ | $y^2$ |
|---|---|---|
| $x$ | $x^2$ | $xy$ |

$x^2 + 2xy + y^2$

$x + y$

The parallel in arithmetic for 15 x 15 is shown at the right.

| 5 | 50 | 25 |
|---|---|---|
| 10 | 100 | 50 |

$10 + 5$

The application of the algebraic algorithm to the multiplication of mixed numbers together with its graphical representation is shown in the next examples. By using a grid in which the area of a 12 x 12 region represents 1, the pictures of mixed fractions with denominators of 2, 3, 4, 6, and 12 (factors of 12) are readily displayed.

Note that the areas of the four regions correspond to the four sub-products created when the algebraic algorithm is used.

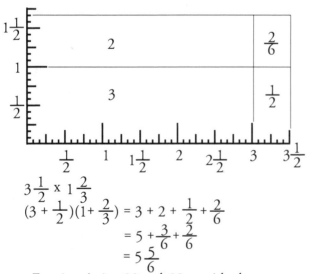

$3\frac{1}{2} \times 1\frac{2}{3}$

$(3 + \frac{1}{2})(1 + \frac{2}{3}) = 3 + 2 + \frac{1}{2} + \frac{2}{6}$

$\qquad = 5 + \frac{3}{6} + \frac{2}{6}$

$\qquad = 5\frac{5}{6}$

$1\frac{1}{3} \times 2\frac{3}{4}$

$(1 + \frac{1}{3})(2 + \frac{3}{4}) = 2 + \frac{3}{4} + \frac{2}{3} + \frac{3}{12}$

$\qquad = 2 + \frac{9}{12} + \frac{8}{12} + \frac{3}{12}$

$\qquad = 2 + \frac{20}{12}$

$\qquad = 3\frac{8}{12}$ or $3\frac{2}{3}$

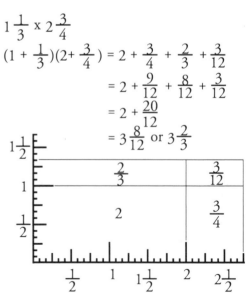

*Fraction Action 88* and *89* provide the opportunity to practice this algorithm and construct the representations.

# Fraction Action 88 – part 1

Please show the multiplication of fractions in two ways as shown in the example:

a. using the distributive property and expanded notation

b. graphically displaying the distributive property process

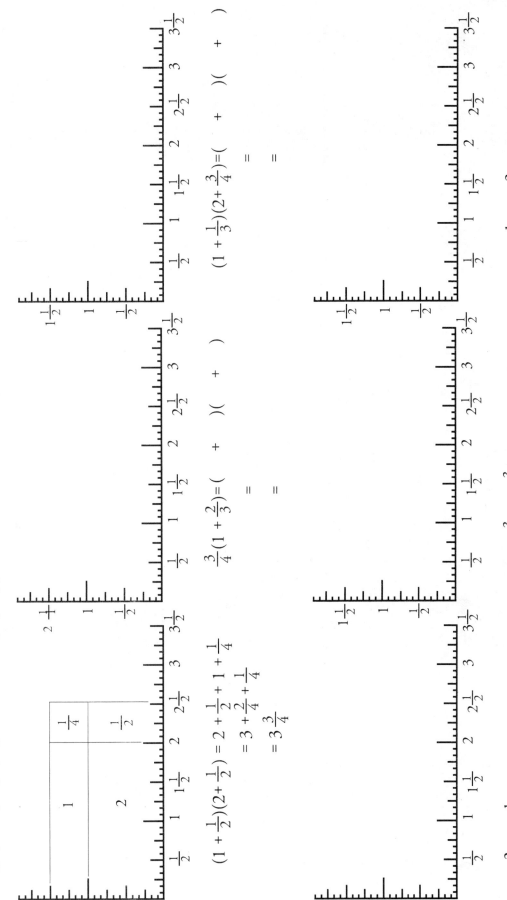

$(1+\frac{1}{2})(2+\frac{1}{2}) = 2 + \frac{1}{2} + 1 + \frac{1}{4}$

$= 3 + \frac{2}{4} + \frac{1}{4}$

$= 3\frac{3}{4}$

$\frac{3}{4}(1+\frac{2}{3}) = (\quad + \quad)(\quad + \quad)$

$=$

$=$

$(1+\frac{1}{3})(2+\frac{3}{4}) = (\quad + \quad)(\quad + \quad)$

$=$

$=$

$\frac{2}{3}(1+\frac{1}{2}) = (\quad + \quad)(\quad + \quad)$

$=$

$=$

$(1+\frac{3}{4})(1+\frac{3}{4}) = (\quad + \quad)(\quad + \quad)$

$=$

$=$

$(1+\frac{1}{4})(2+\frac{2}{3}) = (\quad + \quad)(\quad + \quad)$

$=$

$=$

# Fraction Action 88 – part 2

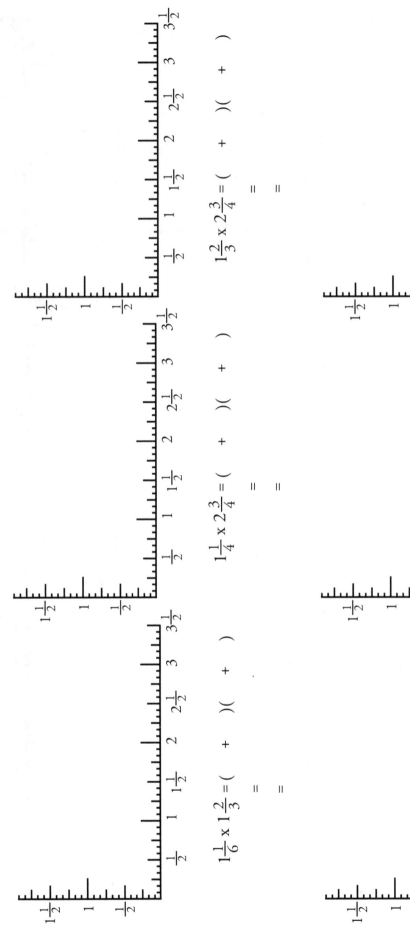

$1\frac{1}{6} \times 1\frac{2}{3} = ( \quad + \quad )( \quad + \quad )$

$=$

$=$

$1\frac{1}{4} \times 2\frac{3}{4} = ( \quad + \quad )( \quad + \quad )$

$=$

$=$

$1\frac{2}{3} \times 2\frac{3}{4} = ( \quad + \quad )( \quad + \quad )$

$=$

$=$

$1\frac{1}{2} \times 2\frac{1}{3} = ( \quad + \quad )( \quad + \quad )$

$=$

$=$

$1\frac{3}{4} \times 2\frac{1}{4} = ( \quad + \quad )( \quad + \quad )$

$=$

$=$

$1\frac{2}{3} \times 2\frac{1}{2} = ( \quad + \quad )( \quad + \quad )$

$=$

$=$

# Fraction Action 89 – part 1

Please show the multiplication of fractions in two ways:

a. using the distributive property and expanded notation
b. graphically displaying the distributive property process

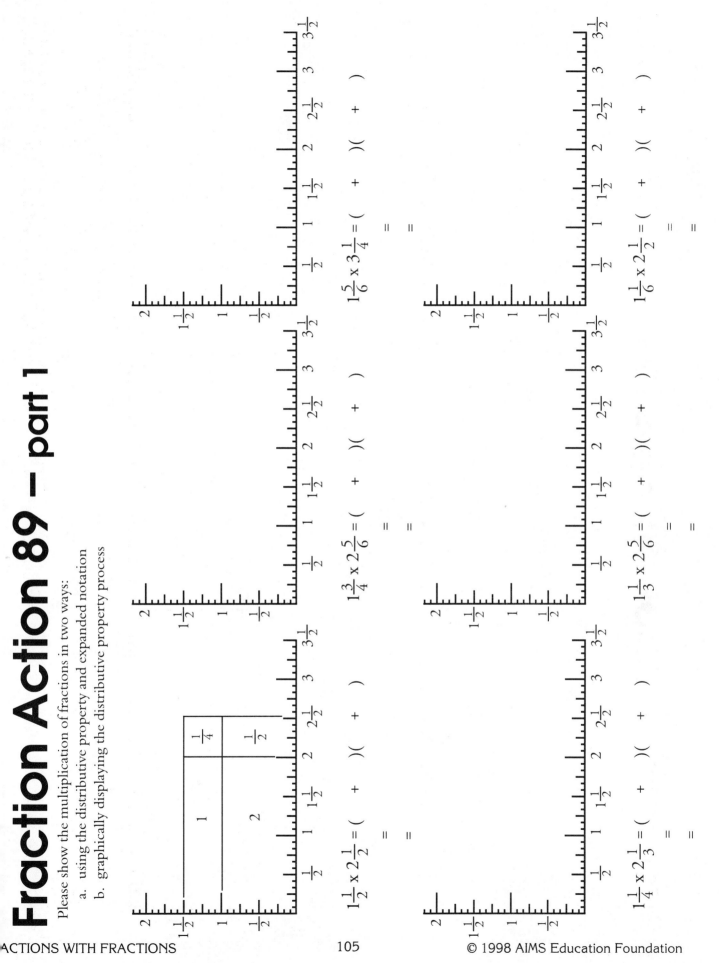

$1\frac{1}{2} \times 2\frac{1}{2} = ( \quad + \quad )( \quad + \quad )$

$=$

$=$

$1\frac{3}{4} \times 2\frac{5}{6} = ( \quad + \quad )( \quad + \quad )$

$=$

$=$

$1\frac{5}{6} \times 3\frac{1}{4} = ( \quad + \quad )( \quad + \quad )$

$=$

$=$

$1\frac{1}{4} \times 2\frac{1}{3} = ( \quad + \quad )( \quad + \quad )$

$=$

$=$

$1\frac{1}{3} \times 2\frac{5}{6} = ( \quad + \quad )( \quad + \quad )$

$=$

$=$

$1\frac{1}{6} \times 2\frac{1}{2} = ( \quad + \quad )( \quad + \quad )$

$=$

$=$

105

# Fraction Action 89 – part 2

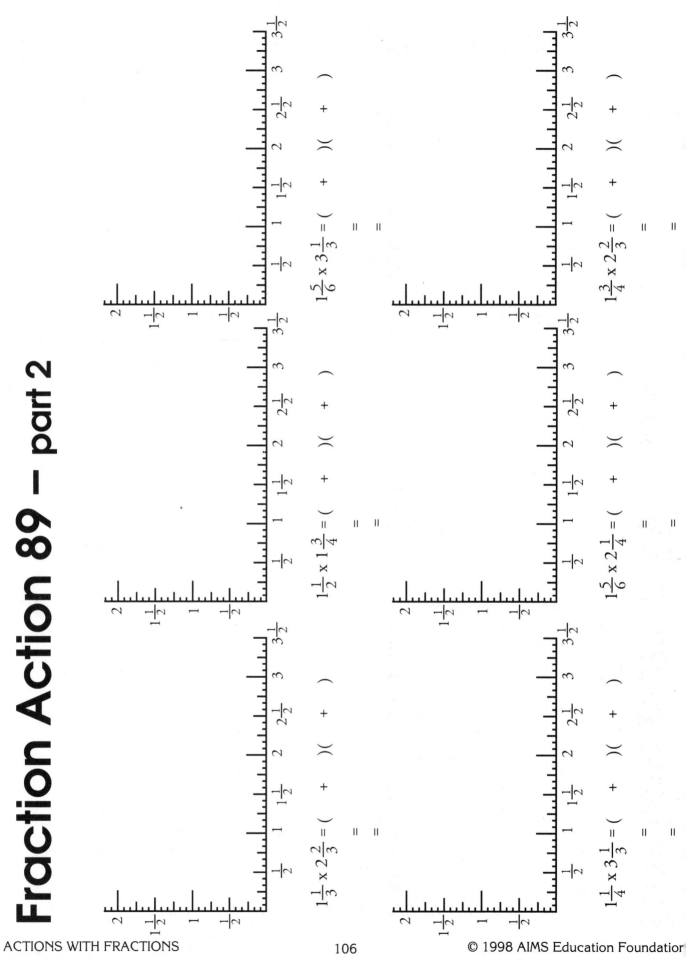

$1\frac{1}{3} \times 2\frac{2}{3} = ( \quad + \quad )( \quad + \quad )$

$=$

$=$

$1\frac{1}{2} \times 1\frac{3}{4} = ( \quad + \quad )( \quad + \quad )$

$=$

$=$

$1\frac{5}{6} \times 3\frac{1}{3} = ( \quad + \quad )( \quad + \quad )$

$=$

$=$

$1\frac{1}{4} \times 3\frac{1}{3} = ( \quad + \quad )( \quad + \quad )$

$=$

$=$

$1\frac{5}{6} \times 2\frac{1}{4} = ( \quad + \quad )( \quad + \quad )$

$=$

$=$

$1\frac{3}{4} \times 2\frac{2}{3} = ( \quad + \quad )( \quad + \quad )$

$=$

$=$

# Division of Fractions Without Inverting

Possibly the most unusual and least understood algorithm in mathematics is the "invert and multiply" approach to the division of fractions. It makes no sense to most students and they use it only in blind obedience to a memorized rule. It is a major source of error for many.

There are mathematicians who argue that division of fractions in itself is of little value. The rare occasions for application of this process in the real world are often better served by other more life-like approaches.

However, since division of fractions will continue to be part of the curriculum, it is interesting to ask whether it is necessary to use the "invert and multiply" algorithm. The answer is no! Described here is an algorithm that is much more straight forward and less confusing.

Take for example the problem: $\dfrac{3}{4} \div \dfrac{1}{2}$

If we divide numerator by numerator and denominator by denominator the result is $\dfrac{3}{2}$. No renaming is necessary as with "inverting and multiplying" in which the result is $\dfrac{6}{4}$.

But, you might argue, this is a special case. That is correct. However, it is possible to make every problem a special case through the use of equivalent fractions. For example:

$$\dfrac{5}{8} \div \dfrac{3}{4}$$

The denominators work but the numerators require 5 to be divided by 3. If $\dfrac{5}{8}$ is replaced by its equivalent $\dfrac{15}{24}$, the division is simple:

$$\dfrac{15}{24} \div \dfrac{3}{4} = \dfrac{5}{6}$$

Notice what happened. Both numerator and denominator of the dividend were multiplied by 3. This resulted in a quotient of $\dfrac{5}{6}$. Had the invert and multiply algorithm been used, the initial quotient would have been $\dfrac{20}{24}$, not $\dfrac{5}{6}$.

An even more challenging situation exists in problems such as:

$$\dfrac{5}{7} \div \dfrac{2}{3}$$

Neither the numerator nor denominator division results in a whole number. However, if both are multiplied by 2 and by 3 (the numerator and denominator of the divisor), everything simplifies:

$$\dfrac{2 \times 3 \times 5}{2 \times 3 \times 7} \div \dfrac{2}{3} = \dfrac{30}{42} \div \dfrac{2}{3} = \dfrac{15}{14} = 1\dfrac{1}{14}$$

Note, especially, that both the numerator and the denominator of the divisor have been inserted as factors of the numerator and denominator of the dividend.

Since renaming to produce equivalent fractions is used regularly in the addition and subtraction of fractions, it is more natural to continue its use in the division of fractions to simplify what students must learn. Further, since all the other operations are consistent (adding in addition, subtracting in subtraction, multiplying in multiplication), it would seem to be advantageous to remain consistent in division by dividing rather than inverting and multiplying. This alternative algorithm reinforces the key role of equivalent fractions.

# Fraction
# Action 90

A straight forward way to divide fractions is to divide the numerator and denominator of the dividend by the numerator and denominator of the divisor, respectively. This can always be done by renaming the dividend so its numerator is a multiple of the divisor numerator and its denominator is a multiple of the divisor denominator.

In your solutions please show the same steps as those in the examples.

Examples:
$$\frac{2}{3} \div \frac{3}{4} =$$

$$\frac{24}{36} \div \frac{3}{4} = \frac{8}{9}$$

$$\frac{1}{4} \div \frac{3}{8} =$$

$$\frac{6}{24} \div \frac{3}{8} = \frac{2}{3}$$

1. $\frac{1}{4} \div \frac{3}{8} =$

2. $\frac{5}{6} \div \frac{1}{3} =$

3. $\frac{3}{8} \div \frac{1}{4} =$

4. $\frac{1}{3} \div \frac{2}{5} =$

5. $\frac{5}{9} \div \frac{2}{3} =$

6. $\frac{1}{6} \div \frac{1}{2} =$

7. $\frac{3}{4} \div \frac{1}{3} =$

8. $\frac{1}{4} \div \frac{5}{6} =$

9. $\frac{2}{3} \div \frac{1}{6} =$

10. $\frac{7}{8} \div \frac{3}{4} =$

11. $\frac{4}{5} \div \frac{2}{3} =$

12. $\frac{5}{8} \div \frac{1}{3} =$

*Part* **7**

# Equivalent Fractions As Proportional Reasoning

Proportional reasoning is a fundamental mathematical process. An important application is in the formation of equivalent fractions. Equivalent fractions are proportionality statements that play a key role in operations such as the addition and subtraction of fractional numbers. Such operations require the renaming of fractional numbers to be of the *same kind*. Renaming employs proportional reasoning.

Proportional reasoning is described in the NCTM publication *Curriculum and Evaluation Standards for School Mathematics* as "of such great value that it merits whatever time and effort must be expended to assure its careful development. Students need to see many problem situations that can be modeled and then solved through proportional reasoning."

The *Mathematics Framework for California Schools* identifies three unifying ideas for the middle grades: *proportional reasoning and relationships, multiple representations, patterns and generalizations.* "These are not specific subjects to be covered only at particular times; rather, they are themes that are present continually, integrating the different things students are learning."

Lesh, Post, and Behr, writing in the NCTM publication *Number Concepts and Operations in the Middle Grades,* stress that "We view proportional reasoning as a pivotal concept. On the one hand, it is the capstone of children's elementary school arithmetic; on the other hand, it is the cornerstone of all that is to follow. ... It therefore occupies a pivotal position in school mathematics."

Given its central role in mathematics, how can we best nurture proportional reasoning? The appropriate response is to make full use of every opportunity where proportional reasoning is involved, pointing out its role, and discussing how it helps to make connections and build understanding. The study of equivalent fractions in the rich contexts of the multiplication table and coordinate graphs provides an excellent opportunity. The invaluable experiences and associations these environments provide belong to the mathematical heritage of every student.

# Equivalent Fractions and the Multiplication Table

*Proportional reasoning involves a purely multiplicative relationship.* It should come as no great surprise that the multiplication table is a table of proportions. Since equivalent fractions are statements of proportionality, it is reasonable to expect that the multiplication table imbeds sets of equivalent fractions. And so it is!

Student understanding of the singular relationship between multiplication and proportional reasoning will help them avoid a frequent error: mixing addition and multiplication in the formulation of proportions. Like oil and water, these operations cannot be mixed in this context. The purely multiplicative nature of proportional reasoning must be preserved.

The multiplication table may be built in one of two ways: in the traditional form or as occurring in the first quadrant of the coordinate plane. The latter is used in activities originating from the AIMS Algebra Project. It has the advantage of consistently providing the same orientation as that used in algebra.

Nevertheless, the traditional form is still useful in selected instances where it provides the appropriate orientation. The activity that follows is one such an instance. Here the traditional form has two advantages: the activity takes place in a context with which the students are familiar, and *proper* fractions are readily identified in the table. When read in the same manner, the first quadrant table would present improper fractions.

Students should be given abundant opportunity to search the multiplication table for patterns before being introduced to those discussed here. Reliance on the multiplication table as a crutch to avoid mastering basic multiplication facts is to be discouraged. However, studying the table for patterns should be encouraged with equal diligence!

The table is so rich in patterns waiting to be discovered that it would be unfortunate if students were to be deprived of this experience. One approach that has met with success is to have students engage in the search for patterns over an extended period of time, periodically posting and sharing discoveries. Each new discovery tends to motivate students to search for others.

Only two of the many patterns are considered here because they apply to proportions in a very particular way. Refer to the multiplication table as you engage in your own search for patterns.

| x | 1 | 2 | 3 | 4 | 5 | 6 | 7 | 8 | 9 |
|---|---|---|---|---|---|---|---|---|---|
| 1 | 1 | 2 | 3 | 4 | 5 | 6 | 7 | 8 | 9 |
| 2 | 2 | 4 | 6 | 8 | 10 | 12 | 14 | 16 | 18 |
| 3 | 3 | 6 | 9 | 12 | 15 | 18 | 21 | 24 | 27 |
| 4 | 4 | 8 | 12 | 16 | 20 | 24 | 28 | 32 | 36 |
| 5 | 5 | 10 | 15 | 20 | 25 | 30 | 35 | 40 | 45 |
| 6 | 6 | 12 | 18 | 24 | 30 | 36 | 42 | 48 | 54 |
| 7 | 7 | 14 | 21 | 28 | 35 | 42 | 49 | 56 | 63 |
| 8 | 8 | 16 | 24 | 32 | 40 | 48 | 56 | 64 | 72 |
| 9 | 9 | 18 | 27 | 36 | 45 | 54 | 63 | 72 | 81 |

Think of the Row 1 entries as numerators and their counterparts in Row 2 as denominators. It is immediately apparent that the fractions formed in this manner are $\frac{1}{2}$ and its equivalents up to $\frac{9}{18}$.

| 1 | 1 | 2 | 3 | 4 | 5 | 6 | 7 | 8 | 9 |
|---|---|---|---|---|---|---|---|---|---|
| 2 | 2 | 4 | 6 | 8 | 10 | 12 | 14 | 16 | 18 |

Test this with other consecutive rows.

But rows need not be consecutive. For example, if Row 2 is thought of as containing numerators and Row 7 the respective denominators, the fractional numbers formed are the equivalents of $\frac{2}{7}$.

| 2 | 2 | 4 | 6 | 8 | 10 | 12 | 14 | 16 | 18 |
|---|---|---|---|---|---|---|---|---|---|
| 7 | 7 | 14 | 21 | 28 | 35 | 42 | 49 | 56 | 63 |

Proper fractions are formed whenever the numerator row lies above the denominator row. Improper fractions are formed whenever the numerator row lies below the denominator row. In the instance of $\frac{7}{5}$, the equivalents are found by thinking of Row 7 as consisting of numerators and Row 5 as denominators.

| 7 | 7 | 14 | 21 | 28 | 35 | 42 | 49 | 56 | 63 |
|---|---|---|---|---|---|---|---|---|---|
| 5 | 5 | 10 | 15 | 20 | 25 | 30 | 35 | 40 | 45 |

The proportional nature of the multiplication table becomes even more apparent using a second approach. In this instance, a rectangle is drawn anywhere in the table with sides parallel to the table boundaries.

| x | 1 | 2 | 3 | 4 | 5 | 6 | 7 | 8 | 9 |
|---|---|---|---|---|---|---|---|---|---|
| 1 | 1 **A** | 2 | 3 | 4 | 5 | 6 | 7 | 8 | 9 |
| 2 | 2 | 4 | 6 | 8 | 10 | 12 | 14 | 16 | 18 |
| 3 | 3 | 6 | 9 | 12 | 15 | 18 **B** | 21 | 24 | 27 |
| 4 | 4 | 8 | 12 | 16 | 20 | 24 | 28 | 32 | 36 |
| 5 | 5 | 10 | 15 | 20 | 25 | 30 | 35 | 40 | 45 |
| 6 | 6 | 12 | 18 | 24 | 30 | 36 | 42 | 48 | 54 |
| 7 | 7 | 14 | 21 | 28 | 35 | 42 | 49 | 56 | 63 |
| 8 | 8 | 16 | 24 | 32 | 40 | 48 | 56 | 64 | 72 |
| 9 | 9 | 18 | 27 | 36 | 45 | 54 | 63 | 72 | 81 |

Study the four numbers in the corners of Rectangle A before reading further:

$$1 \qquad 5$$

$$4 \qquad 20$$

It becomes obvious that these can be viewed as the equivalent fractions $\frac{1}{4}$ and $\frac{5}{20}$. They can also be viewed as another set of equivalent fractions: $\frac{1}{5}$ and $\frac{4}{20}$. The relationship can be expressed as proportions in several ways:

$$1 : 5 = 4 : 20$$
$$1 : 4 = 5 : 20$$

Finally, the cross-products are equal: $1 \times 20 = 4 \times 5$. Note, particularly, the multiplicative relationships that permeate this array. Five-twentieths is derived from $\frac{1}{4}$ by multiplying its numerator and denominator by 5, $\frac{4}{20}$ is derived from $\frac{1}{5}$ by multiplying by 4, and the cross-products are equal. These relationships are the hallmark of all proportions.

Rectangle B has a different orientation. In this instance the numbers in the corner are:

$$18 \qquad 24$$

$$48 \qquad 64$$

It is readily apparent that the fractional numbers $\frac{18}{48}$ and $\frac{24}{64}$ are equivalent and both are equivalents of $\frac{3}{8}$; further, $\frac{18}{24}$ and $\frac{48}{64}$ are equivalent and both are equivalents of $\frac{3}{4}$. What is not so apparent is how $\frac{24}{64}$ is derived from $\frac{18}{48}$ through multiplication. However, if both numerator and denominator of $\frac{18}{48}$ are multiplied by $\frac{4}{3}$ the result is $\frac{24}{64}$. Similarly, $\frac{48}{64}$ is the result of multiplying the numerator and denominator of $\frac{18}{24}$ by $\frac{8}{3}$.

The multiplicative relationships in proportions should be underscored constantly. The disaster that results from using the additive relationship with proportions is made evident by testing the addition table using both of the procedures described above. It is suggested that students test the addition table in this manner to implant the fact that addition must never be put into the mix when working with proportions. Researchers have found such mixing to be the chief cause of error students make in formulating proportions. *Fraction Action 91* encourages students to explore proportions imbedded in the multiplication table.

# Fraction Action 91

Please draw a rectangle enclosing different sets of numbers in the body of each multiplication table. The sides of the rectangle must be parallel to the boundaries of the table. In each rectangle, examine the numbers in the four corners for a pattern. Please make a record of your findings. Is there a pattern? Does it always hold?

|   | 1 | 2 | 3 | 4 | 5 | 6 | 7 | 8 | 9 |
|---|---|---|---|---|---|---|---|---|---|
| 1 | 1 | 2 | 3 | 4 | 5 | 6 | 7 | 8 | 9 |
| 2 | 2 | 4 | 6 | 8 | 10 | 12 | 14 | 16 | 18 |
| 3 | 3 | 6 | 9 | 12 | 15 | 18 | 21 | 24 | 27 |
| 4 | 4 | 8 | 12 | 16 | 20 | 24 | 28 | 32 | 36 |
| 5 | 5 | 10 | 15 | 20 | 25 | 30 | 35 | 40 | 45 |
| 6 | 6 | 12 | 18 | 24 | 30 | 36 | 42 | 48 | 54 |
| 7 | 7 | 14 | 21 | 28 | 35 | 42 | 49 | 56 | 63 |
| 8 | 8 | 16 | 24 | 32 | 40 | 48 | 56 | 64 | 72 |
| 9 | 9 | 18 | 27 | 36 | 45 | 54 | 63 | 72 | 81 |

|   | 1 | 2 | 3 | 4 | 5 | 6 | 7 | 8 | 9 |
|---|---|---|---|---|---|---|---|---|---|
| 1 | 1 | 2 | 3 | 4 | 5 | 6 | 7 | 8 | 9 |
| 2 | 2 | 4 | 6 | 8 | 10 | 12 | 14 | 16 | 18 |
| 3 | 3 | 6 | 9 | 12 | 15 | 18 | 21 | 24 | 27 |
| 4 | 4 | 8 | 12 | 16 | 20 | 24 | 28 | 32 | 36 |
| 5 | 5 | 10 | 15 | 20 | 25 | 30 | 35 | 40 | 45 |
| 6 | 6 | 12 | 18 | 24 | 30 | 36 | 42 | 48 | 54 |
| 7 | 7 | 14 | 21 | 28 | 35 | 42 | 49 | 56 | 63 |
| 8 | 8 | 16 | 24 | 32 | 40 | 48 | 56 | 64 | 72 |
| 9 | 9 | 18 | 27 | 36 | 45 | 54 | 63 | 72 | 81 |

|   | 1 | 2 | 3 | 4 | 5 | 6 | 7 | 8 | 9 |
|---|---|---|---|---|---|---|---|---|---|
| 1 | 1 | 2 | 3 | 4 | 5 | 6 | 7 | 8 | 9 |
| 2 | 2 | 4 | 6 | 8 | 10 | 12 | 14 | 16 | 18 |
| 3 | 3 | 6 | 9 | 12 | 15 | 18 | 21 | 24 | 27 |
| 4 | 4 | 8 | 12 | 16 | 20 | 24 | 28 | 32 | 36 |
| 5 | 5 | 10 | 15 | 20 | 25 | 30 | 35 | 40 | 45 |
| 6 | 6 | 12 | 18 | 24 | 30 | 36 | 42 | 48 | 54 |
| 7 | 7 | 14 | 21 | 28 | 35 | 42 | 49 | 56 | 63 |
| 8 | 8 | 16 | 24 | 32 | 40 | 48 | 56 | 64 | 72 |
| 9 | 9 | 18 | 27 | 36 | 45 | 54 | 63 | 72 | 81 |

|   | 1 | 2 | 3 | 4 | 5 | 6 | 7 | 8 | 9 |
|---|---|---|---|---|---|---|---|---|---|
| 1 | 1 | 2 | 3 | 4 | 5 | 6 | 7 | 8 | 9 |
| 2 | 2 | 4 | 6 | 8 | 10 | 12 | 14 | 16 | 18 |
| 3 | 3 | 6 | 9 | 12 | 15 | 18 | 21 | 24 | 27 |
| 4 | 4 | 8 | 12 | 16 | 20 | 24 | 28 | 32 | 36 |
| 5 | 5 | 10 | 15 | 20 | 25 | 30 | 35 | 40 | 45 |
| 6 | 6 | 12 | 18 | 24 | 30 | 36 | 42 | 48 | 54 |
| 7 | 7 | 14 | 21 | 28 | 35 | 42 | 49 | 56 | 63 |
| 8 | 8 | 16 | 24 | 32 | 40 | 48 | 56 | 64 | 72 |
| 9 | 9 | 18 | 27 | 36 | 45 | 54 | 63 | 72 | 81 |

# Part 8 — Equivalent Fractions and the Coordinate Plane

One way of displaying fractional numbers is to graph them on the number line. For example, the point representing $\frac{1}{2}$ is graphed at the midpoint between 0 and 1. This is useful in that it portrays the measure of $\frac{1}{2}$ in comparison to that of 1. But it can be located properly only if the underlying understanding already exists and, therefore, it does little to enhance understanding.

$$0 \qquad\qquad \frac{1}{2} \qquad\qquad 1$$

When the equivalents of $\frac{1}{2}$ are graphed on the same number line, they stack up at the same location like characters on a totem pole. No differentiation is provided. This togetherness masks much that is of interest about equivalent fractions. Further, it is difficult to accurately graph fractions such as $\frac{3}{5}$, $\frac{5}{7}$, and $\frac{2}{9}$, making this approach practically useless for comparing and ordering all but the simplest fractions. The limited meaning associated with this approach does little to excite student interest and enhance the learning experience.

In contrast, graphing fractional numbers on the coordinate plane creates a wealth of understandings and connections. Fractional numbers are graphed on the coordinate plane using the ordered pairs (denominator, numerator). The value of the denominator is located on the horizontal axis and that of the numerator on the vertical axis. Denominators speak of *what kind* and numerators of *how many*. The order (denominator, numerator) is of vital importance and must be maintained since significant mathematical concepts are imbedded as a result.

Vizualizing fractional numbers by graphing them on the coordinate plane greatly expands and enriches meaning. It provides another model that is superior to other models in certain instances. Each new model brings to the table additional meaning.

The first discovery students may make when using this approach is that each fractional number has a *unique location or address!* No more totem pole stacking! A second and very important discovery is that the graphs of a given set of equivalent fractions are points belonging to the same straight line! Among other discoveries, students may make are the following:

- the line connecting graphs of equivalent fractions always passes through the origin,
- the slope of any such line is named by the equivalent fractions graphed on it,
- the integer point graphed nearest the origin is the fraction expressed in lowest terms,
- the tangent function of the angle formed by such a line and the horizontal axis is named by the equivalent fractions graphed on it,
- extending the line to pass over 100 on the horizontal axis permits direct reading of the equivalent percent.

An appropriate manipulative model for this type of graphing is readily constructed. It consists of three elements: a pegboard (available at home building supply stores), golf tees, and rubber bands. The most useful pegboard size has a 13 x 13 hole array. It permits graphing fractions with denominators up to 12. If small wood blocks of uniform thickness are glued underneath the four corners, the pegboard will have enough clearance to permit insertion of the golf tees. This pegboard has a major advantage over those geoboards with protrusions in that only those points under consideration are marked by the golf tees. This focuses all attention on the fractions under study.

The graphs of $\frac{1}{2}$ and $\frac{3}{4}$ graphed as the ordered pairs (2, 1) and (4, 3) are illustrated below.

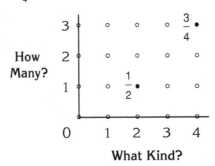

What about the equivalents of $\frac{1}{2}$? How is this type of graph superior to that on the number line? As shown below, each fractional number has a unique address and the graph of this set of equivalents are points of the same line! Notice that $\frac{1}{2}$, $\frac{2}{4}$, $\frac{3}{6}$, and $\frac{4}{8}$ are graphed in this illustration.

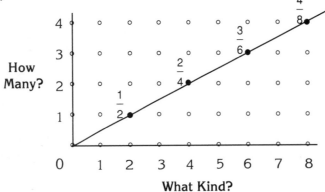

That these fractions belong to the same "family" is evidenced by their arrangement as points of the same line. This particular line will henceforth bear the designation "one-half line." Note that it passes through the **origin**. *The line through the graph of any set of equivalents will always pass through the origin.* Since the line is infinite in length, it contains the graphs of all equivalents of one-half! Those graphed at lattice points (or holes in the geoboard) are simple fractions and those located between lattice points are compound fractions.

The *slope* of the one-half line is 50% or $\frac{1}{2}$. Slope is defined as the ratio of *rise/run*. *Rise* is the distance above the horizontal axis and is measured vertically. *Run* is the distance from the vertical axis and is measured horizontally. The one-half line rises half the distance that it recedes horizontally from the origin.

Common **misconceptions** exist about slopes such as:
- a line with a 50% slope rises at a 45° angle, and
- a vertical line has a slope of 100%.

Neither is true. A study of the illustration shows that the line making a 45° angle with the horizontal has a 100% slope! A vertical line has an infinite slope. Slopes of lines running through the origin and passing through the first quadrant range from zero to infinity and include all values between.

But there is more! The *tangent value* of the angle formed by the one-half line and the horizontal axis is $\frac{1}{2}$ or 0.5! Therefore, the line passing through a set of equivalent fractions has a slope that is numerically equal to the tangent value and the set of equivalent fractions. This assists students in building understanding of and appreciation for these interrelationships.

# Comparing Fractional Numbers

A further advantage of coordinate plane graphing over number line graphing lies in the fact that it is easy to **accurately** graph fractions such as $\frac{3}{5}$, $\frac{5}{7}$, and $\frac{2}{9}$. If lines are drawn passing through their addresses and the origin, the slopes become evident and can be readily compared. The greater the slope, the greater the fraction. For example, the fractions $\frac{2}{5}$ and $\frac{3}{8}$ are compared below.

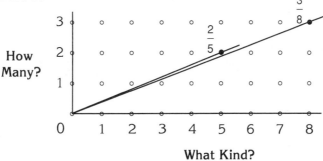

Note again that the slope of the horizontal axis is zero and of the vertical axis is infinite. Every number, positive or negative, is associated with the slope of a line through the origin and every slope is associated with a number. Since every positive number lies between zero and infinity, the line with an equivalent slope will pass through the first quadrant, the origin, and third quadrant. Similarly, a line whose slope is negative will pass through the second quadrant, origin, and fourth quadrant. This provides a graph for every rational and irrational number.

During the entire time students are using this approach to graphing, they are a developing powerful mental imagery of fractional numbers and their interrelationships. The representations on the geoboard or a dot array on paper provide manipulative and visual experiences that fortify this mental imagery. *Fraction Action 92* provides student experiences with this approach to the study of equivalent fractions.

# Finding the Lowest Common Multiple
# for Adding and Subtracting Fractions

Graphing on the coordinate plane provides a revealing look at the concept of lowest common multiple. As fractions are graphed, they are automatically sorted by *kind* since each column represents a different kind. Halves appear above Column 2, fifths above Column 5, etc. Two different kinds of fraction never appear in the same column.

Suppose that we want to add $\frac{1}{2}$, $\frac{2}{3}$, and $\frac{1}{4}$. These fractions represent three different *kinds* of fractional parts: halves, thirds, and fourths. The number of objects can be added only if they are of the same kind. Therefore, it becomes necessary to look at equivalents to find out whether a common kind exists among them. Considered in ascending order, the first occurance where equivalents of all three appear in the same column determines the lowest common multiple of the denominators and the lowest common denominator (or kind) of the three fractions.

Following is the graphical approach to determining common multiples. Each fraction and several of its equivalents are graphed, a process through which they are *sorted by kind*. *Fractions whose graphs or addresses are located in the same column are of the same kind.*

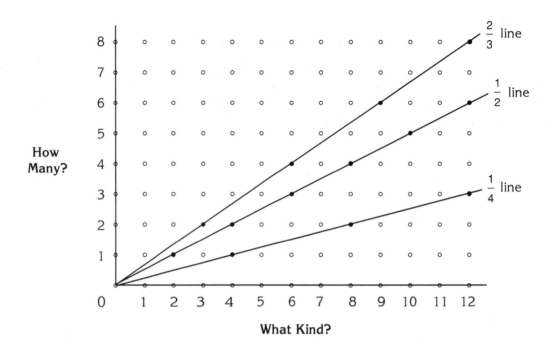

Scanning from left to right, the first column to contain the graphs of two fractions is 4. Their kind is fourths and 4 is the lowest common denominator for $\frac{1}{2}$ and $\frac{1}{4}$. The next occurance is above 6. The two fractions with addresses in this column are $\frac{1}{2}$ and $\frac{2}{3}$. Six is the lowest common denominator for $\frac{1}{2}$ and $\frac{2}{3}$.

The first column containing the graphs of all three fractions is 12. Therefore, 12 is the lowest common multiple of 2, 3, and 4, and the lowest common denominator for $\frac{1}{2}$, $\frac{2}{3}$, and $\frac{1}{4}$. The equivalents in Column 12 are $\frac{6}{12}$, $\frac{8}{12}$, and $\frac{3}{12}$. Since they are now of the *twelfths kind*, they can be added: 6 + 8 + 3 twelfths or 17 twelfths.

On the grid or geoboard, fractions are added by *stacking their heights* one on top of the other. The respective heights are 6, 8, and 3 units and their combined height is 17 units. The result can be read from the geoboard:

How high? Seventeen units.

What kind? Twelfths.

Similarly, the difference of two fractions of the same kind is found by determining the *difference in their heights.* Consider the example $\frac{1}{2} - \frac{1}{3}$.

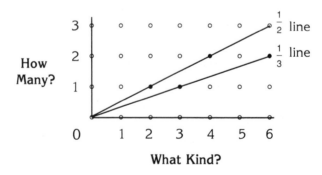

The first column that contains their equivalents is 6 and the kind is sixths. Here the $\frac{1}{2}$ line is 3 units high and the $\frac{1}{3}$ line is 2 units high. The difference is 1 unit, $\frac{1}{2} - \frac{1}{3} = \frac{1}{6}$.

# The Multiplicative Inverse

The product of a fractional number and its multiplicative inverse is 1 as in $\frac{2}{5}$ x $\frac{5}{2}$ = 1. This raises the conjecture that 1 plays an interesting role in this relationship. Let's study this matter by first constructing the 1-line and then graphing $\frac{2}{5}$ and $\frac{5}{2}$.

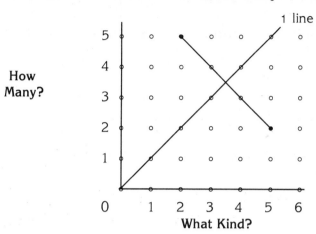

Next, a line segment connecting $\frac{2}{5}$ and $\frac{5}{2}$ is drawn. What relationship does this line segment have with the 1-line?

The following graph shows several additional sets of multiplicative inverses: $\frac{2}{7}$ and $\frac{7}{2}$, $\frac{3}{4}$ and $\frac{4}{3}$, $\frac{4}{9}$ and $\frac{9}{4}$, and $\frac{3}{8}$ and $\frac{8}{3}$.

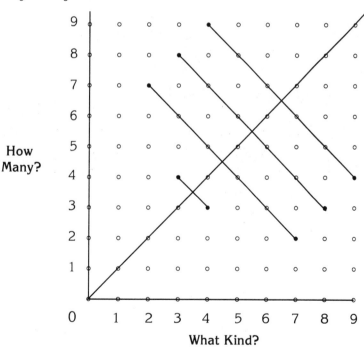

*The line segment connecting each set of multiplicative inverses has two relationships to the 1-line: it is perpendicular to the 1-line and bisected by it.* This makes it easy to graph the multiplicative inverse of any fractional number on such a geoboard or grid: let the 1-line serve as a mirror. Locate the image of the graph of a fraction and it will be at the address of the multiplicative inverse.

It is interesting to consider how a mirror and the 1-line are related. When you look at your image in a mirror, you see yourself rotated through 180° about a vertical axis. The right hand now appears as the left hand. Similarly, the fraction is turned through 180° about the one-line to display the multiplicative inverse!

## Three Regions of the Plane

The 1-line divides the coordinate plane into three regions: the area below, the area above, and the 1-line itself. Anything on the 1-line is equivalent to 1 or 100%. Fractional numbers graphed below this line are known as proper fractions with a value less than one. Fractional numbers graphed above this line are known as improper fractions with a value greater than 1.

## Converting Fractions to Percent

Can this graphical approach by used to change fractions to percents or percents to fractions? Statements involving percents are proportions of the kind:

$$\frac{a}{b} = \frac{c}{100}$$

This can be read as "the numerator is to the unknown percent as the denominator is to 100 percent." a and c relate to the part; b and 100 to the whole. For example, if $\frac{3}{5}$ is to be converted into a percent we use the proportion:

$$\frac{3}{5} = \frac{c}{100}$$

On the graph or geoboard a rule divided into 100 units is located along the 10 column as shown. Its top ends at $\frac{10}{10}$ or the 1-line. The ruler measures distances or heights above the horizontal axis in one percent units.

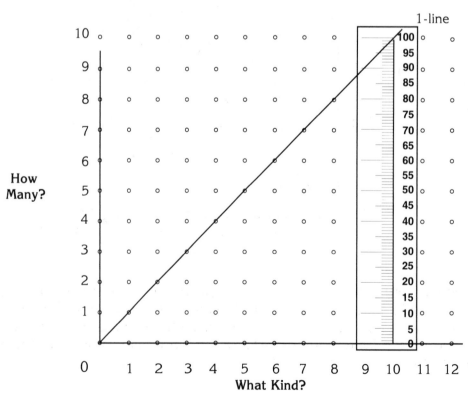

First graph the fraction. Then draw a line through the origin and the fraction so it crosses the ruler. Where the line crosses the ruler, read the decimal equivalent.

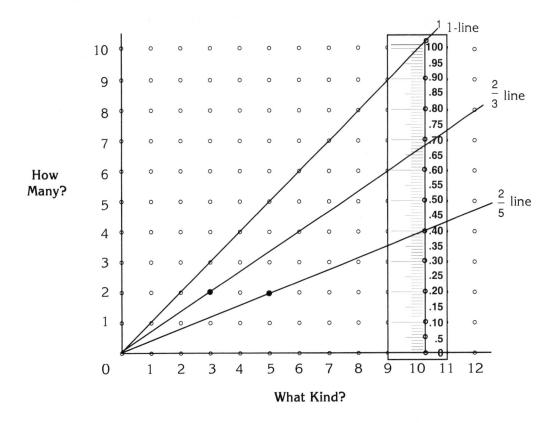

In this example the $\frac{2}{5}$ line passes through .40 on the ruler. Two-fifths = 0.4. Two-thirds passes through a point between 0.66 and 0.67. If drawn with great precision, it will be closer to 0.67 than 0.66 and will round to 0.67.

Since there is always error connected with either the placement of the ruler or drawing of the line, the results will be approximate. The greater the precision of both, the greater the accuracy. Nevertheless, the process of conversion is exemplified graphically.

# Converting Percents to Fractions

To convert a percent to a fraction, follow an inverse procedure. Locate the desired percent on the ruler and connect that point with the origin. If the line segment passes through any point on its way to the origin, that point is the address of an equivalent fraction. If it does not pass through any point, then any point close to the line will be the address of a fraction that is approximately equivalent.

In this graph the line segment connecting 75% and the origin passes through the intersections named by the ordered pairs (8, 6) and (4, 3), the graphs of $\frac{6}{8}$ and $\frac{3}{4}$, respectively. In contrast, the line segment connecting 45% and the origin does not pass through any intersection. It runs just below the points (8, 4), (6, 3), (4, 2), and (2, 1). Therefore, 45% is less than $\frac{1}{2}$ but more than $\frac{3}{5}$, for example. It is closest to $\frac{4}{9}$.

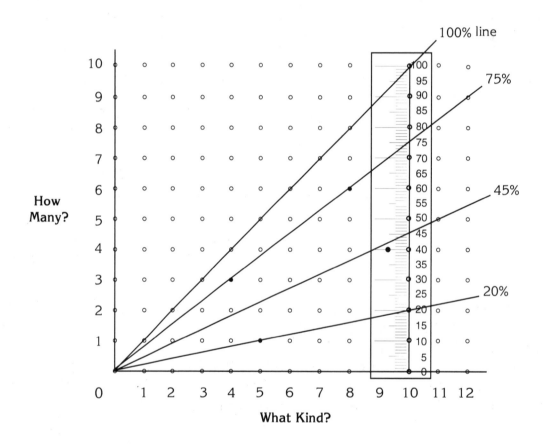

The 20% line runs through the point (5, 1) and is therefore equivalent to $\frac{1}{5}$. In summary, the graph can indicate an approximate or exact fractional number equivalent.

# Fractions and Decimals

The only difference between converting fractions to percents and converting to decimals lies in the construction of the ruler. Instead of being sub-divided into percents it is sub-divided into hundredths.

# Fraction Action 92
## Patterns in Equivalent Fractions

*Fraction Action 92* helps students focus on the graphical determination of equivalent fractions, their relative magnitudes, and their lowest common denominators. It is truly remarkable that so much relevant content flows naturally out of graphing fractions on the coordinate plane!

Equivalent fractions graphed on the coordinate plane are *always* points of the same straight line. This line always passes through the origin. In a *simple fraction,* the numerator and denominator are whole numbers. *In a set of equivalent fractions, the simple fraction in lowest terms is the one nearest the origin!* As a result, this activity permits students to rename a fraction in lowest terms geometrically.

The "steepness" of a line graphing a set of equivalent fractions is a measure of the common magnitude. It is also referred to as the slope. *The steeper the line, the greater the slope and the greater the magnitude of the fraction.* Students are asked to rank-order these fractions using this knowledge.

It is interesting to note that the horizontal axis has a zero slope, the vertical axis has an infinite slope, and the fraction $\frac{1}{1}$ or "1-line" has a slope of 45 degrees. Any fraction that graphs between the 1-line and the vertical axis is an improper fraction and every fraction that graphs between the 1-line and the horizontal axis is a proper fraction.

Another interesting result of graphing fractions becomes evident when the dots marking intersections crossed by the fraction lines are studied. Each such event locates an equivalent fraction. If all the dots for the four lines have been marked correctly, the following are true:

- If no dots occur in a column, then the column number is not a factor of any of the denominators.
- If one dot occurs, the column number is a factor of only one of these denominators.
- If two dots occur, the column number is the common denominator for those two fractions on whose lines these dots appear.
- If three or more dots occur, the column number is the common denominator for those fractions on whose lines these dots appear.

*The column nearest the origin containing two or more dots is the lowest common denominator for the fractions involved.*

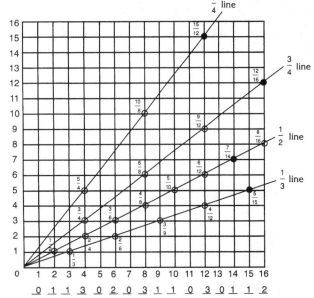

Answer to h:

$$\frac{5}{4} > \frac{3}{4} > \frac{1}{2} > \frac{1}{3}$$

# Fraction
# Action 92

Use a small closed circle to show the plot of these fractions on the coordinate plane: $\frac{7}{14}$, $\frac{5}{15}$, $\frac{12}{16}$, and $\frac{15}{12}$. Connect each plot to the origin with a line drawn *very carefully*.

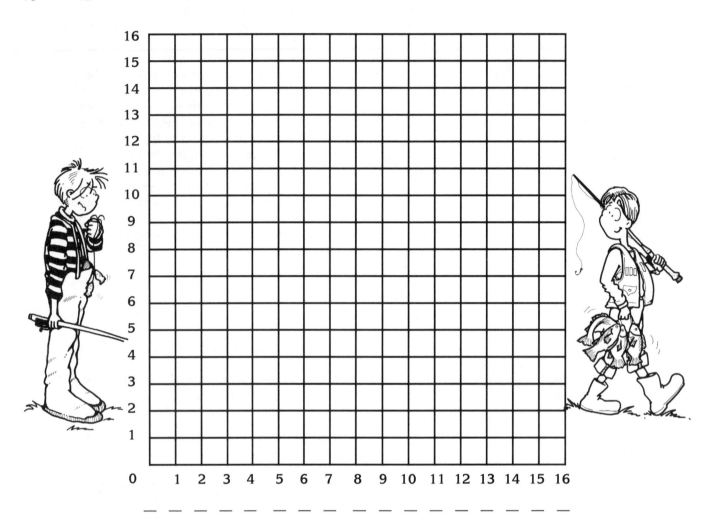

a. Do any lines pass through intersections? If so, mark them with a small open circle. In the spaces underneath the graph, record the number of dots you have drawn in each column.

b. Do the marked intersections have any special significance? Please explain.

c. If any of your dots are the "homes" of fractions, please label them with their names.

# Fraction
# Action 92

d. Arrange any equivalent fractions you named in descending order (greatest numerator and denominator to least).

$$\frac{7}{14} =$$        $$\frac{5}{15} =$$        $$\frac{12}{16} =$$        $$\frac{15}{12} =$$

e. Where, along each line, do you find the fraction that is expressed in lowest terms?

f. Describe how graphing can be used to locate equivalent fractions and to identify the fraction that is expressed in lowest terms?

g. How is the steepness of the line related to the magnitude of the fraction?

h. Name each of the four lines using the equivalent fraction expressed in lowest terms as the label. Arrange the four line names in order from the greatest to the least.

i. Examine the columns and the dots you marked. Do any of the columns contain no dots? ... one dot? ... two dots? ... three dots? Do these results have meaning? Please explain.

    1. No dots

    2. One dot

    3. Two dots

    4. Three or more dots

# Fraction Action 93
# The Parade of Triplets

In this activity each fraction is graphed as the ordered pair (denominator, numerator). With this approach every fraction has a unique "home" on the coordinate plane and equivalent fractions are different points of the same line. For example, the fraction $\frac{1}{2}$ and its equivalents are graphed as the ordered pairs (2, 1), (4, 2), (6, 3), (8, 4), etc. A straight line can be drawn that passes through all of these points and the origin. Such a line can be variously described as having a slope (or grade) of 50% or a slope of $\frac{1}{2}$. We can refer to it as the 50% line, $\frac{1}{2}$ line, or 0.5 line.

This activity illuminates the relationship existing among decimal fractions, ordinary fractions, and percents. While not included, the slope (or grade, in the case of roads) also belongs in this relationship. The slope is actually made visible by the lines students draw in the activity. Slope or grade is normally expressed as a percent.

The goal of the activity is to make a visual impact on students of these interrelationships. A feeling of power comes from drawing the lines and seeing them pass through points that are graphs of equivalent fractions.

The "1-line" is key in such graphs. It passes through $\frac{1}{1}$, $\frac{2}{2}$, $\frac{3}{3}$, etc. dividing the plane into three parts: the 1-line, the space below and the space above it. The space below is where proper fractions and percents less than 100% are graphed. The space above is where improper fractions and percents greater than 100% are graphed.

The 100% scale on the student page begins at 10 on the horizontal axis and reaches to 1.0 on the 1-line. It can be extended for percentages greater than 100. The point 10 on the horizontal axis was selected because it is the most convenient and meaningful for building the scale. Any other point could be used but since the top of the 100% scale must terminate on the 1-line, other choices would be less convenient and desireable. Once the end points are determined, the connecting line segment is divided into 100 parts to obtain one percent units.

It needs to be emphasized that the lines should be drawn as accurately as possible to have the desired impact. When a line appears to pass through a point on the graph, it is circled to show that it determines an equivalent fraction or a fraction that is very nearly equivalent. Only 33% and 67% are in the latter category. When the line clearly does not pass through any point, the students are asked to find the point closest to the line and record it as the nearest fraction equivalent. In this activity $\frac{1}{7}$ lies closest to the 0.15 line and $\frac{4}{9}$ is nearest to the 0.45 line, shown by arrows.

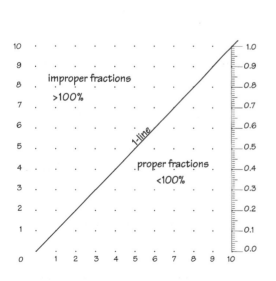

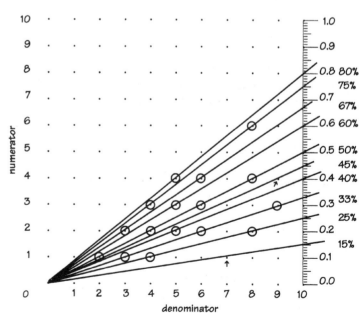

# Fraction
# Action 93

Certain numbers are commonly expressed in one of three forms: decimal fractions, percents, and fractions. Because of the frequency with which they are interrelated in the real world, it is important to understand them as triplets.

In this activity you will use the coordinate plane to which a decimal fraction ruler has been added to graphically determine the relationships which name the triplets. With this approach there will be instances in which the results are approximate. In such cases, find the closest fraction equivalent.

Please use this procedure:
1. Find the desired decimal fraction on the scale.
2. From this determine the percent equivalent.
3. Carefully draw a line connecting the point on the scale to the origin.
4. Locate the graphs of fraction equivalents through which this line passes or the closest fraction equivalent if the line does not pass through a point. Record the results.

| Decimal Fraction | Percent Equivalent | Fraction Equivalent(s) | Closest Fraction Equivalent |
|---|---|---|---|
| 0.80 | | | |
| 0.60 | | | |
| 0.25 | | | |
| 0.50 | | | |
| 0.75 | | | |
| 0.40 | | | |
| 0.15 | | | |
| 0.45 | | | |
| 0.33 | | | |
| 0.67 | | | |

# Fraction
# Action 93

| 10 | · | · | · | · | · | · | · | · | · | · | — 1.0 |
| 9 | · | · | · | · | · | · | · | · | · | · | — 0.9 |
| 8 | · | · | · | · | · | · | · | · | · | · | — 0.8 |
| 7 | · | · | · | · | · | · | · | · | · | · | — 0.7 |
| 6 | · | · | · | · | · | · | · | · | · | · | — 0.6 |
| 5 | · | · | · | · | · | · | · | · | · | · | — 0.5 |
| 4 | · | · | · | · | · | · | · | · | · | · | — 0.4 |
| 3 | · | · | · | · | · | · | · | · | · | · | — 0.3 |
| 2 | · | · | · | · | · | · | · | · | · | · | — 0.2 |
| 1 | · | · | · | · | · | · | · | · | · | · | — 0.1 |
| 0 | · | · | · | · | · | · | · | · | · | · | — 0.0 |

0   1   2   3   4   5   6   7   8   9   10

# Part 9

# Explorations with the Addition of Fractions

*AIMS Mathematical Microworlds* constitute an approach to the study of mathematics that permits students to experience the essence of what it means to "do" mathematics. Each topic explored in a microworld is sufficiently restricted in scope for its content and processes to be comprehensible. As multiple microworlds are explored, their interrelationships become apparent and the breadth of understanding grows.

It is hoped that by exploring numerous mathematical microworlds, students will come to construct an understanding of mathematics and the nature of doing mathematics that is both meaningful and reasonably broad.

## What is an AIMS Mathematical Microworld?

One way to understand an AIMS Mathematical Microworld is to use an analogy that compares it with how a nation is structured and relates to other nations. All nations have certain essential characteristics that mark their existence and interrelationships. These essentials have their counterparts in mathematical microworlds.

### Territory

The world is subdivided into nations and every nation occupies a defined territory except where there are border disputes. The inhabitants in each nation are typically engaged in exploring its resources and potential. In the same way each microworld constitutes a defined territory of mathematics that is limited in scope.

For example, the coordinate plane forms the territory in which the action in *Part Nine* of this publication takes place. Students have the opportunity to explore what happens if fractions are graphed on the coordinate plane using the ordered pairs (denominator, numerator). As they explore and discover, the vast potential of the coordinate plane microworld becomes clear.

### Citizens

Every nation defines citizenship, making it possible to identify citizens. In *Part Nine* the "citizens" are fractions living on the coordinate plane. Their homes can be located using their coordinate pair addresses (denominator, numerator). The fraction citizens engage in a broad range of activities, such as belonging to a club of equivalent fractions, all of whom live on the same straight line.

### Laws and Regulations

Order in a nation is maintained by the observation of laws and regulations. For fractions in the coordinate plane environment, the fundamental principle underlying all laws is that every fraction has a home that it shares with no other fraction. Observation of this fundamental law of the land makes it possible to "do" significant mathematics and make numerous valuable discoveries.

## Fraction Puzzles

In addition to the Microworlds, two fraction puzzles are included in this section.

## National Goals

Each nation establishes its values and goals, usually imbedding them in its constitution. In the same manner, each microworld specifies the specific primary pursuit in which its citizens are to engage. The primary pursuit in mathematical microworlds is to explore every nook and cranny within its territory. Just as within any society, discoveries are to be celebrated and shared.

The territory, citizens, laws and regulations, and national goals set the stage for problem-solving expeditions that go far beyond the use of arithmetic algorithms. Citizens may use trial and error, hypothesis making, analysis of emerging patterns, synthesis, logic, inductive and deductive reasoning, arriving at generalizations, and other higher-order thinking skills in the process of making discoveries.

## International Relations

No nation is an island to itself, isolated from the world. In the same way, no mathematical microworld is without a multitude of connections to other microworlds. In the exploration of a microworld, processes and content are clarified and before long common elements among microworlds become evident. Content is often discovered to connect in significant ways to other microworlds. Thus the meaning of such content is enriched through being viewed in the context of multiple microworlds. Processes learned in one context are found to be applicable in other contexts. As a result inter-microworld bonds develop, "international" understanding increases, and the vision of the world of mathematics is broadened and made more comprehensible.

## *Fraction Action 94 – 98*

*Fraction Action 94 – 98* utilize one type of mathematical microworld in which the sums along two or more rows of fractions are to be the same. Spaces in the rows are connected by segments of a straight line.

The design constitutes the territory. The sets of fraction names are the citizens. The law states that each fraction is used once and only once and the sum along each row must be the same. The goal is to find all possible solutions for each set of citizens. The number of possible solutions is not indicated by the number of spaces for reporting discoveries. There may be more or fewer solutions than the spaces would indicate.

The activities assume that students can add simple fractions mentally or with reasonable facility use paper and pencil.

Here are three solutions for *Fraction Action 94* using the first set of fractions:

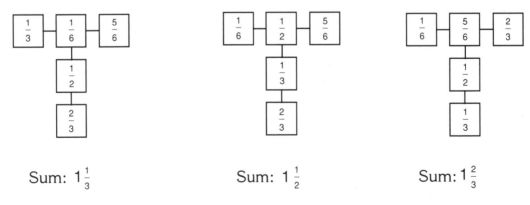

Sum: $1\frac{1}{3}$     Sum: $1\frac{1}{2}$     Sum: $1\frac{2}{3}$

Further search will show that the sum of $1\frac{1}{3}$ is the minimum and the sum of $1\frac{2}{3}$ is the maximum possible. Other solutions in this section are left for the students (and teacher) to discover.

By using cutouts of the fractions found in the *Appendix*, the fractions can be moved about without leaving a trace of error. Students will generally begin these explorations by using trial and error. Eventually, they will discover other secrets that help them to quickly identify the range of answers and all possible answers.

## Fraction Activities 99 – 101

These activities take place in another mathematical microworld named *Blockout*. The objective is to combine adjoining cells (those sharing a common side) whose fractions have a sum of 1. Correct and incorrect patterns are shown below. All of the *Blockouts* have solution and some may have more than one solution. All of the fractions will have been included in a subgroup with a sum of 1 if the correct pattern is found. Here is an example drawn from *Fraction Action 100*:

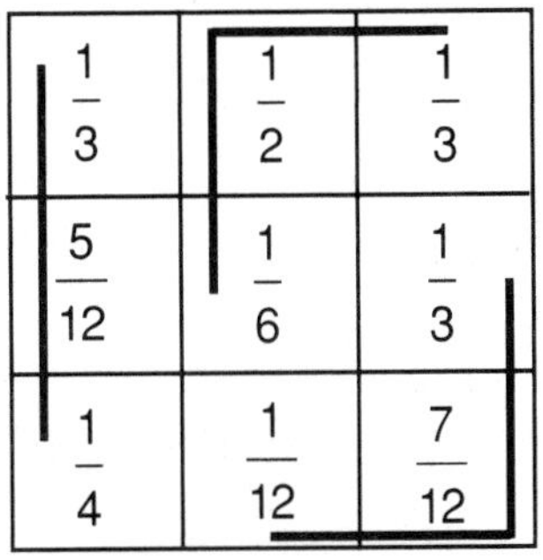

| $\frac{1}{3}$ | $\frac{1}{2}$ | $\frac{1}{3}$ |
|---|---|---|
| $\frac{5}{12}$ | $\frac{1}{6}$ | $\frac{1}{3}$ |
| $\frac{1}{4}$ | $\frac{1}{12}$ | $\frac{7}{12}$ |

*Correct Pattern*

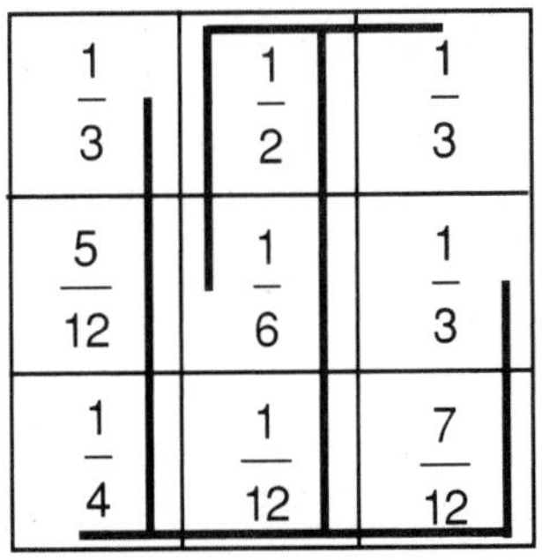

| $\frac{1}{3}$ | $\frac{1}{2}$ | $\frac{1}{3}$ |
|---|---|---|
| $\frac{5}{12}$ | $\frac{1}{6}$ | $\frac{1}{3}$ |
| $\frac{1}{4}$ | $\frac{1}{12}$ | $\frac{7}{12}$ |

*Incorrect Pattern*

# Fraction Action 94
## The Little T

Is it possible to arrange the fractions $\frac{1}{6}$, $\frac{1}{3}$, $\frac{1}{2}$, $\frac{2}{3}$, and $\frac{5}{6}$ in the following design so that the sum along each of the two arms is the same? If so, is more than one such sum possible?

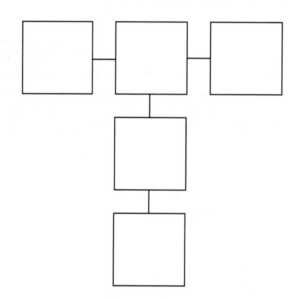

**Please make a record of any solutions in the spaces provided.**

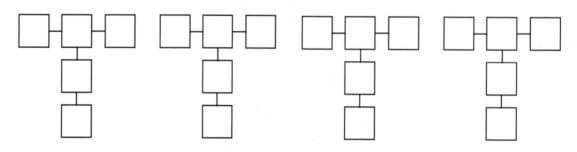

Is it possible to arrange the fractions $\frac{1}{8}$, $\frac{1}{4}$, $\frac{3}{8}$, $\frac{1}{2}$, and $\frac{5}{8}$ in this design so that the sum along each of the two arms is the same? If so, is more than one such sum possible?

**Please make a record of any solutions in the spaces provided.**

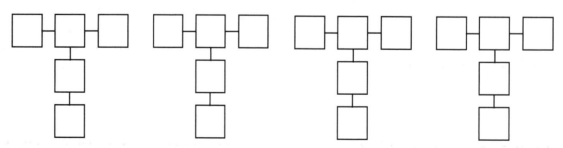

# Fraction Action 95
## The Big T

Is it possible to arrange the fractions $\frac{1}{8}, \frac{1}{4}, \frac{3}{8}, \frac{1}{2}, \frac{5}{8}$, and $\frac{3}{4}$ in the following design so that the sum along each of the two arms is the same?

If so, is more than one solution?

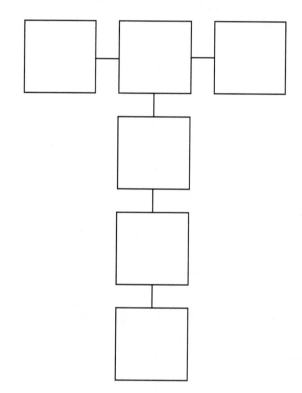

**Please make a record of all your solutions in the spaces provided.**

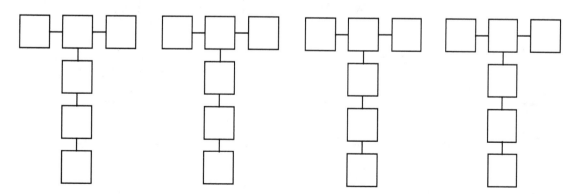

**Please describe any patterns you discovered.**

# Fraction
# Action 96
## The X Design

Is it possible to arrange the fractions $\frac{1}{6}$, $\frac{1}{3}$, $\frac{1}{2}$, $\frac{2}{3}$, and $\frac{5}{6}$ in the following design so that the sum along each of the two arms is the same?

If so, is more than one solution?

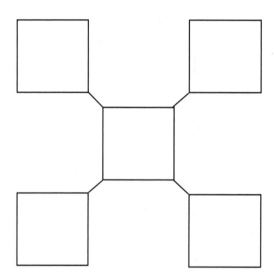

Please make a record of all your solutions in the spaces provided.

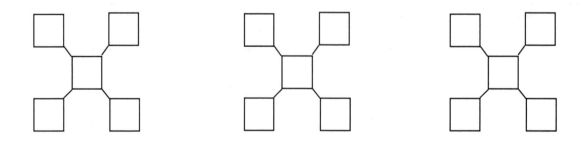

Please describe any patterns you discovered.

# Fraction Action 97

## The U Design

Is it possible to arrange the fractions $\frac{1}{12}$, $\frac{1}{6}$, $\frac{1}{4}$, $\frac{1}{3}$, and $\frac{5}{12}$ in the following design so that the sum along each of the two arms is the same?

If so, is more than one solution?

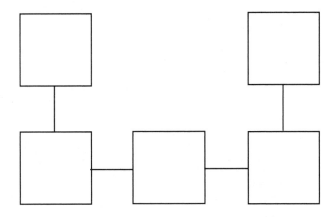

Please make a record of all your solutions in the spaces provided.

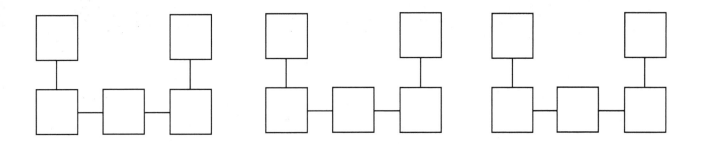

Please describe any patterns you discovered.

134

# Fraction Action 98

## The Ferris Wheel

Is it possible to arrange the fractions $\frac{1}{8}$, $\frac{1}{4}$, $\frac{3}{8}$, $\frac{1}{2}$, $\frac{5}{8}$, $\frac{3}{4}$, and $\frac{7}{8}$ in the following design so that the sum along each of the three arms is the same?

If so, is more than one solution?

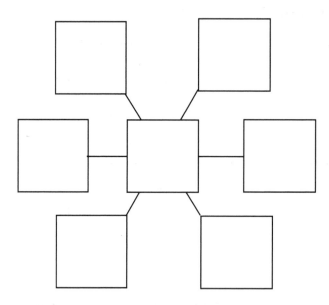

**Please make a record of all your solutions in the spaces provided.**

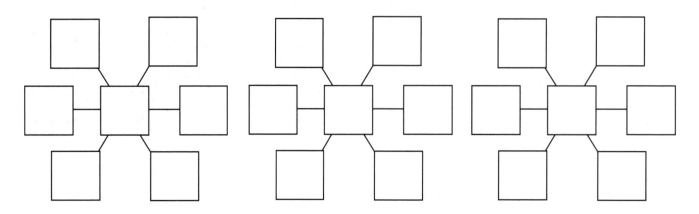

**Please describe any patterns you discovered.**

# Fraction
# Action 99

## Blockout A

The objective of Blockout A is to combine adjoining cells whose fractions have the sum of 1. Each cell in a group must share at least one side with another cell in the same group. Groups cannot overlap. If the proper pattern is used, all fractions will become members of a group.

Correct pattern examples:

Incorrect pattern example:

| $\frac{1}{4}$ | $\frac{1}{4}$ | $\frac{1}{2}$ |
|---|---|---|
| $\frac{1}{4}$ | $\frac{1}{4}$ | $\frac{1}{4}$ |
| $\frac{1}{4}$ | $\frac{3}{4}$ | $\frac{1}{4}$ |

| $\frac{1}{2}$ | $\frac{1}{8}$ | $\frac{1}{2}$ |
|---|---|---|
| $\frac{3}{8}$ | $\frac{1}{8}$ | $\frac{3}{8}$ |
| $\frac{1}{4}$ | $\frac{5}{8}$ | $\frac{1}{8}$ |

| $\frac{1}{6}$ | $\frac{1}{3}$ | $\frac{1}{2}$ |
|---|---|---|
| $\frac{1}{6}$ | $\frac{1}{2}$ | $\frac{1}{6}$ |
| $\frac{1}{6}$ | $\frac{1}{3}$ | $\frac{2}{3}$ |

| $\frac{1}{3}$ | $\frac{1}{3}$ | $\frac{1}{3}$ |
|---|---|---|
| $\frac{1}{2}$ | $\frac{1}{6}$ | $\frac{1}{3}$ |
| $\frac{1}{6}$ | $\frac{2}{3}$ | $\frac{1}{6}$ |

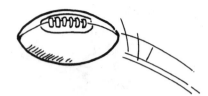

# Fraction Action 100

## Blockout B

The objective of Blockout B is to combine adjoining cells whose fractions have the sum of 1. Each cell in a group must share at least one side with another cell in the same group. Groups cannot overlap. If the proper pattern is used, all fractions will become members of a group.

Correct pattern examples:

Incorrect pattern example:

| $\dfrac{1}{3}$ | $\dfrac{1}{2}$ | $\dfrac{1}{3}$ |
|---|---|---|
| $\dfrac{5}{12}$ | $\dfrac{1}{6}$ | $\dfrac{1}{3}$ |
| $\dfrac{1}{4}$ | $\dfrac{1}{12}$ | $\dfrac{7}{12}$ |

| $\dfrac{2}{3}$ | $\dfrac{1}{3}$ | $\dfrac{1}{4}$ |
|---|---|---|
| $\dfrac{1}{12}$ | $\dfrac{1}{6}$ | $\dfrac{5}{12}$ |
| $\dfrac{1}{4}$ | $\dfrac{1}{3}$ | $\dfrac{1}{2}$ |

| $\dfrac{2}{3}$ | $\dfrac{1}{6}$ | $\dfrac{1}{12}$ |
|---|---|---|
| $\dfrac{1}{2}$ | $\dfrac{1}{12}$ | $\dfrac{1}{12}$ |
| $\dfrac{5}{12}$ | $\dfrac{2}{3}$ | $\dfrac{1}{3}$ |

| $\dfrac{1}{12}$ | $\dfrac{1}{3}$ | $\dfrac{1}{4}$ |
|---|---|---|
| $\dfrac{1}{12}$ | $\dfrac{5}{6}$ | $\dfrac{1}{12}$ |
| $\dfrac{7}{12}$ | $\dfrac{5}{12}$ | $\dfrac{1}{3}$ |

# Fraction Action 101

## Blockout C

The objective of Blockout C is to combine adjoining cells whose fractions have the sum of 1. Each cell in a group must share at least one side with another cell in the same group. Groups cannot overlap. If the proper pattern is used, all fractions will become members of a group.

Correct pattern examples:

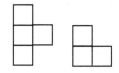

Incorrect pattern example:

| $\dfrac{3}{12}$ | $\dfrac{1}{3}$ | $\dfrac{1}{2}$ | $\dfrac{5}{12}$ |
|---|---|---|---|
| $\dfrac{3}{6}$ | $\dfrac{1}{4}$ | $\dfrac{1}{6}$ | $\dfrac{1}{6}$ |
| $\dfrac{1}{3}$ | $\dfrac{7}{12}$ | $\dfrac{1}{12}$ | $\dfrac{1}{3}$ |
| $\dfrac{1}{12}$ | $\dfrac{6}{12}$ | $\dfrac{1}{3}$ | $\dfrac{1}{6}$ |

| $\dfrac{1}{6}$ | $\dfrac{9}{12}$ | $\dfrac{7}{12}$ | $\dfrac{1}{4}$ |
|---|---|---|---|
| $\dfrac{4}{12}$ | $\dfrac{1}{12}$ | $\dfrac{1}{6}$ | $\dfrac{6}{12}$ |
| $\dfrac{2}{6}$ | $\dfrac{1}{3}$ | $\dfrac{1}{4}$ | $\dfrac{1}{4}$ |
| $\dfrac{1}{6}$ | $\dfrac{1}{4}$ | $\dfrac{1}{3}$ | $\dfrac{1}{4}$ |

# Fraction Action 102 – Puzzle 1

Please design a puzzle that has six pieces, each a different color, constructed with interlocking blocks. The pieces are to be of such a design that they can be formed into a 4 x 6 rectangle. Use 1, 2, 3, 4, 6, and 8 blocks, respectively, for the six pieces. When building the pieces, place any remaining projection pointing upward.

You may find it easier to create the design by first illustrating it on the grid.

Exchange your puzzle with another student. Solve each other's puzzles, find, and record the information asked for in the table. The perimeter is determined by counting each of the outer four edges of the completed puzzle.

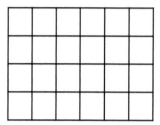

The mass of the completed puzzle is_____grams.

If the puzzle costs 84 cents, find the cost of each of the six pieces.

Please complete the table.

| Color of Part | Fraction Name | Name in Lowest Terms | Predicted Mass | Actual Mass | Cost of Part | Part of Perimeter |
|---|---|---|---|---|---|---|
|  |  |  |  |  |  |  |
|  |  |  |  |  |  |  |
|  |  |  |  |  |  |  |
|  |  |  |  |  |  |  |
|  |  |  |  |  |  |  |
|  |  |  |  |  |  |  |
| Total |  |  |  |  |  |  |

Use this space and the back of this sheet to show your work.

# Fraction Action 103 – Puzzle 2

Please design a puzzle that has six pieces, each a different color, constructed with interlocking blocks. The pieces are to be of such a design that they can be formed into a 6 x 6 rectangle. Use 2, 3, 4, 6, 9, and 12 blocks, respectively, for the six pieces. When building the pieces place any remaining projection pointing upward.

You may find it easier create the design by first illustrating it on the grid. Exchange your puzzle with another student. Solve each other's puzzles, find, and record the information asked for in the table. The perimeter is determined by counting each of the four outer edges of the completed puzzle.

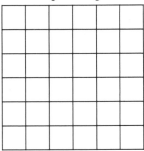

The mass of the completed puzzle is _____ grams.

If the puzzle costs $1.56 cents, find the cost of each of the six pieces.

Please complete the table.

| Color of Part | Fraction Name | Name in Lowest Terms | Predicted Mass | Actual Mass | Cost of Part | Part of Perimeter |
|---|---|---|---|---|---|---|
| | | | | | | |
| | | | | | | |
| | | | | | | |
| | | | | | | |
| | | | | | | |
| Total | | | | | | |

Use this space and the back of this sheet to show your work.

# Appendix

| $\frac{1}{2}$ | $\frac{1}{3}$ | $\frac{1}{4}$ | $\frac{2}{3}$ | $\frac{3}{8}$ | $\frac{1}{12}$ | $\frac{7}{8}$ | $\frac{7}{12}$ |
| $\frac{3}{4}$ | $\frac{1}{6}$ | $\frac{5}{6}$ | $\frac{1}{8}$ | $\frac{5}{8}$ | $\frac{5}{12}$ | $\frac{11}{12}$ | |

| $\frac{1}{2}$ | $\frac{1}{3}$ | $\frac{1}{4}$ | $\frac{2}{3}$ | $\frac{3}{8}$ | $\frac{1}{12}$ | $\frac{7}{8}$ | $\frac{7}{12}$ |
| $\frac{3}{4}$ | $\frac{1}{6}$ | $\frac{5}{6}$ | $\frac{1}{8}$ | $\frac{5}{8}$ | $\frac{5}{12}$ | $\frac{11}{12}$ | |

| $\frac{1}{2}$ | $\frac{1}{3}$ | $\frac{1}{4}$ | $\frac{2}{3}$ | $\frac{3}{8}$ | $\frac{1}{12}$ | $\frac{7}{8}$ | $\frac{7}{12}$ |
| $\frac{3}{4}$ | $\frac{1}{6}$ | $\frac{5}{6}$ | $\frac{1}{8}$ | $\frac{5}{8}$ | $\frac{5}{12}$ | $\frac{11}{12}$ | |

| $\frac{1}{2}$ | $\frac{1}{3}$ | $\frac{1}{4}$ | $\frac{2}{3}$ | $\frac{3}{8}$ | $\frac{1}{12}$ | $\frac{7}{8}$ | $\frac{7}{12}$ |
| $\frac{3}{4}$ | $\frac{1}{6}$ | $\frac{5}{6}$ | $\frac{1}{8}$ | $\frac{5}{8}$ | $\frac{5}{12}$ | $\frac{11}{12}$ | |

| $\frac{1}{2}$ | $\frac{1}{3}$ | $\frac{1}{4}$ | $\frac{2}{3}$ | $\frac{3}{8}$ | $\frac{1}{12}$ | $\frac{7}{8}$ | $\frac{7}{12}$ |
| $\frac{3}{4}$ | $\frac{1}{6}$ | $\frac{5}{6}$ | $\frac{1}{8}$ | $\frac{5}{8}$ | $\frac{5}{12}$ | $\frac{11}{12}$ | |

# Fraction Tiles

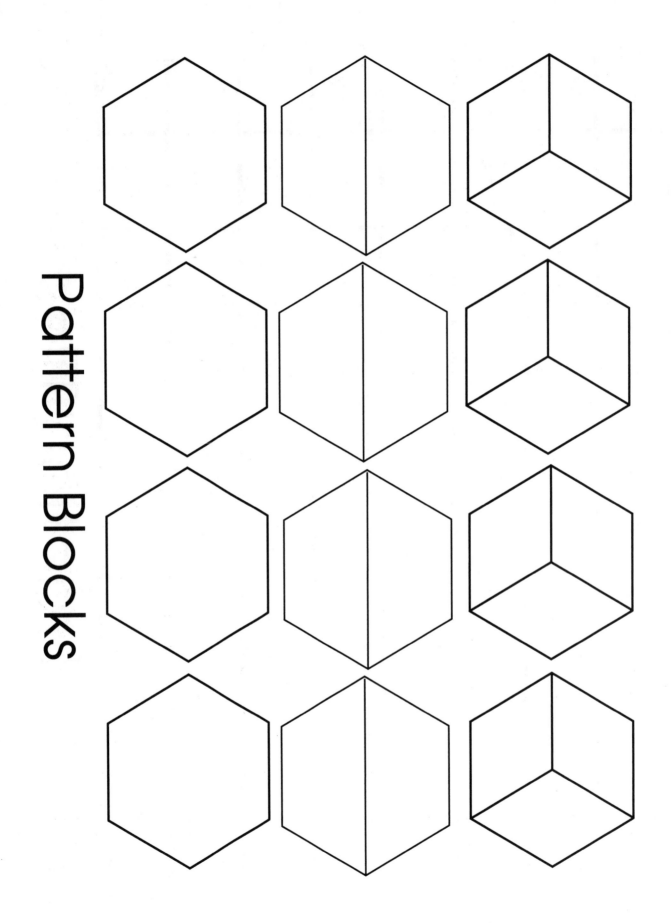

Pattern Blocks

ACTIONS WITH FRACTIONS 143 © 1998 AIMS Education Foundation

# Fraction Squares

Copy the two pages of Unit Squares onto transparency film. Cut out squares. To model the multiplication of fractions, overlay the appropriate dots and stripe squares.

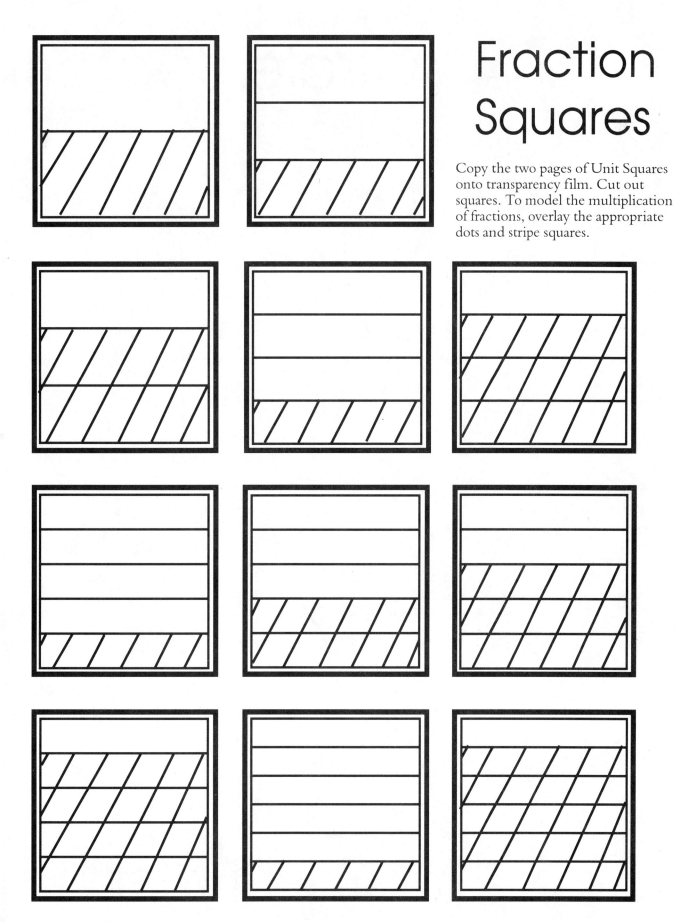

# Fraction
# Squares

Copy the two pages of Unit Squares onto transparency film. Cut out squares. To model the multiplication of fractions, overlay the appropriate dots and stripe squares.

# Circle Sectors

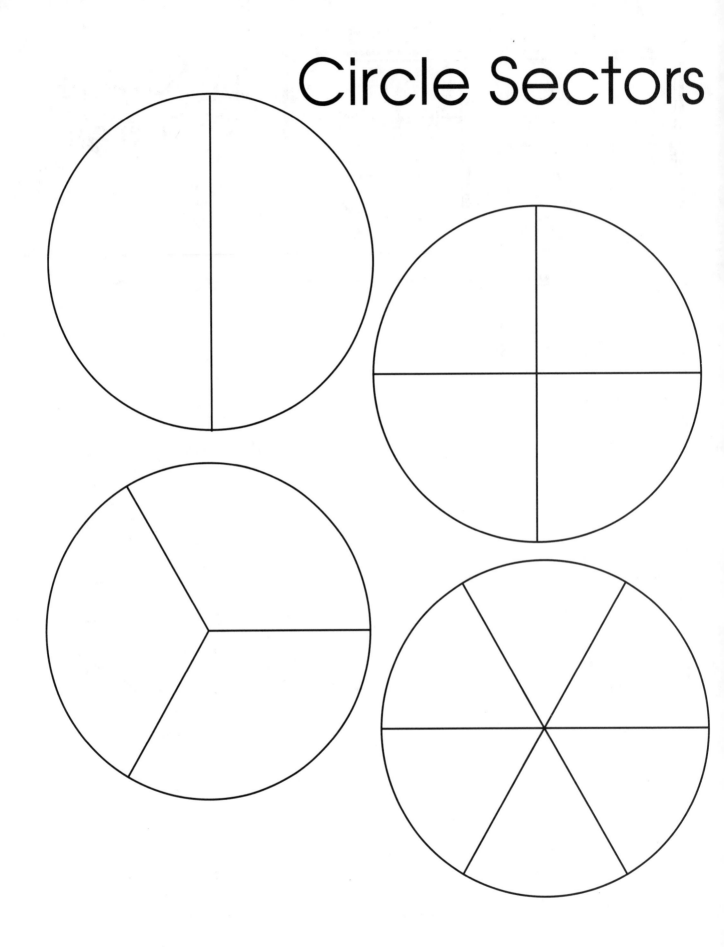

# Circle Sectors

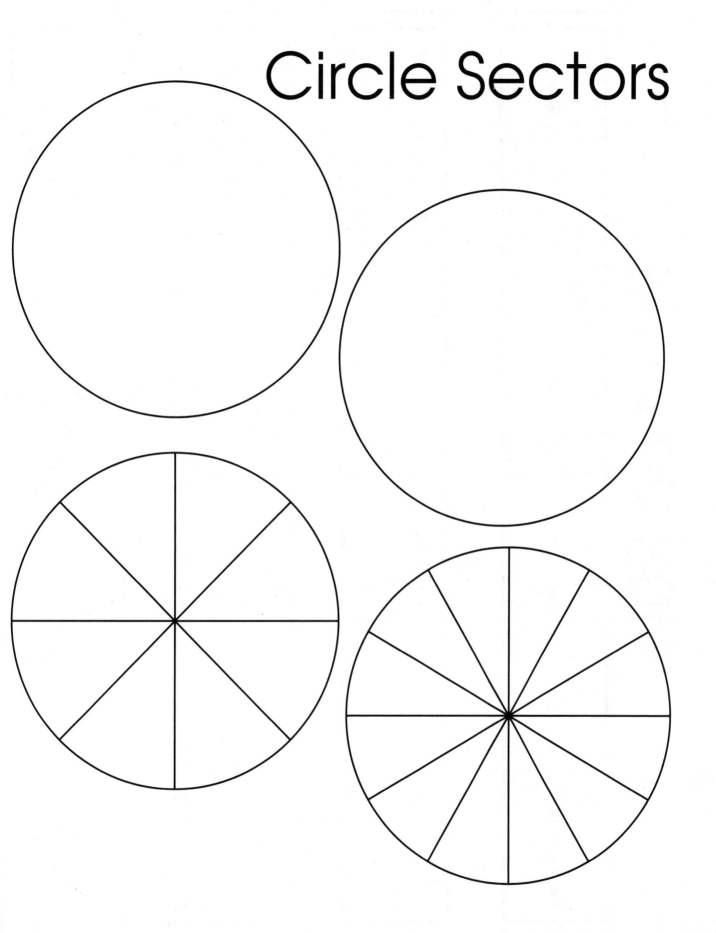

# Fraction Ruler

Ruler 1:

$2$
$\frac{23}{24}$
$\frac{11}{12}$
$\frac{7}{8}$
$\frac{5}{6}$
$\frac{19}{24}$
$\frac{3}{4}$
$\frac{17}{24}$
$\frac{2}{3}$
$\frac{5}{8}$
$\frac{7}{12}$
$\frac{13}{24}$
$\frac{1}{2}$
$\frac{11}{24}$
$\frac{5}{12}$
$\frac{3}{8}$
$\frac{1}{3}$
$\frac{7}{24}$
$\frac{1}{4}$
$\frac{5}{24}$
$\frac{1}{6}$
$\frac{1}{8}$
$\frac{1}{12}$
$\frac{1}{24}$
$1$
$\frac{23}{24}$
$\frac{11}{12}$
$\frac{7}{8}$
$\frac{5}{6}$
$\frac{19}{24}$
$\frac{3}{4}$
$\frac{17}{24}$
$\frac{2}{3}$
$\frac{5}{8}$
$\frac{7}{12}$
$\frac{13}{24}$
$\frac{1}{2}$
$\frac{11}{24}$
$\frac{5}{12}$
$\frac{3}{8}$
$\frac{1}{3}$
$\frac{7}{24}$
$\frac{1}{4}$
$\frac{5}{24}$
$\frac{1}{6}$
$\frac{1}{8}$
$\frac{1}{12}$
$\frac{1}{24}$

(Rulers 2, 3, and 4 are identical to Ruler 1.)

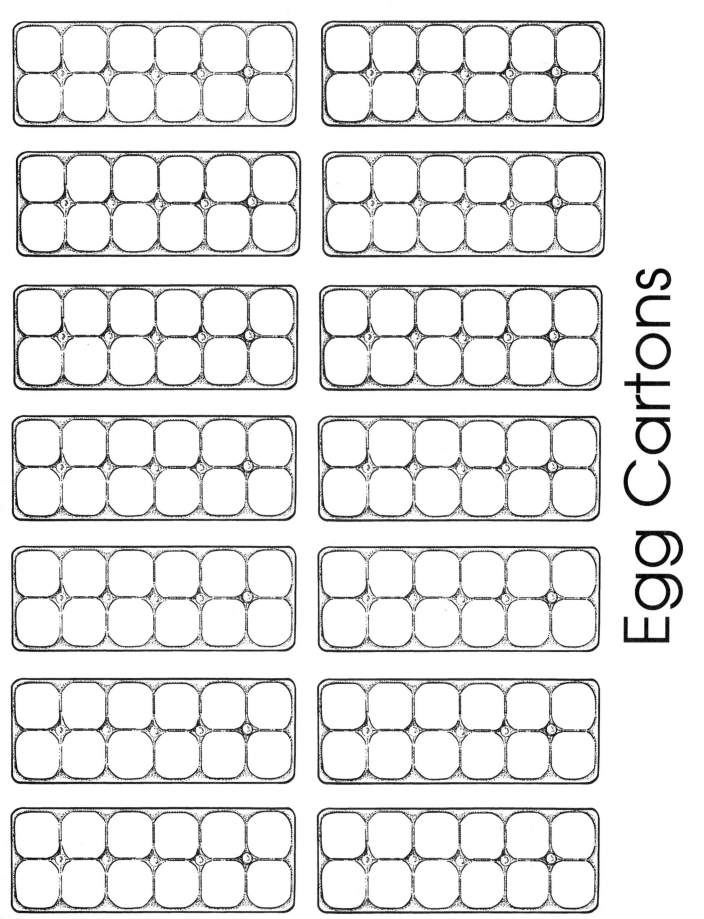

149

Egg Cartons

150

Egg Cartons

# The AIMS Program

AIMS is the acronym for "**A**ctivities **I**ntegrating **M**athematics and **S**cience." Such integration enriches learning and makes it meaningful and holistic. AIMS began as a project of Fresno Pacific University to integrate the study of mathematics and science in grades K-9, but has since expanded to include language arts, social studies, and other disciplines.

AIMS is a continuing program of the non-profit AIMS Education Foundation. It had its inception in a National Science Foundation funded program whose purpose was to explore the effectiveness of integrating mathematics and science. The project directors in cooperation with 80 elementary classroom teachers devoted two years to a thorough field-testing of the results and implications of integration.

The approach met with such positive results that the decision was made to launch a program to create instructional materials incorporating this concept. Despite the fact that thoughtful educators have long recommended an integrative approach, very little appropriate material was available in 1981 when the project began. A series of writing projects have ensued and today the AIMS Education Foundation is committed to continue the creation of new integrated activities on a permanent basis.

The AIMS program is funded through the sale of this developing series of books and proceeds from the Foundation's endowment. All net income from program and products flows into a trust fund administered by the AIMS Education Foundation. Use of these funds is restricted to support of research, development, and publication of new materials. Writers donate all their rights to the Foundation to support its on-going program. No royalties are paid to the writers.

The rationale for integration lies in the fact that science, mathematics, language arts, social studies, etc., are integrally interwoven in the real world from which it follows that they should be similarly treated in the classroom where we are preparing students to live in that world. Teachers who use the AIMS program give enthusiastic endorsement to the effectiveness of this approach.

Science encompasses the art of questioning, investigating, hypothesizing, discovering, and communicating. Mathematics is a language that provides clarity, objectivity, and understanding. The language arts provide us powerful tools of communication. Many of the major contemporary societal issues stem from advancements in science and must be studied in the context of the social sciences. Therefore, it is timely that all of us take seriously a more holistic mode of educating our students. This goal motivates all who are associated with the AIMS Program. We invite you to join us in this effort.

Meaningful integration of knowledge is a major recommendation coming from the nation's professional science and mathematics associations. The American Association for the Advancement of Science in *Science for All Americans* strongly recommends the integration of mathematics, science, and technology. The National Council of Teachers of Mathematics places strong emphasis on applications of mathematics such as are found in science investigations. AIMS is fully aligned with these recommendations.

Extensive field testing of AIMS investigations confirms these beneficial results.

1. Mathematics becomes more meaningful, hence more useful, when it is applied to situations that interest students.
2. The extent to which science is studied and understood is increased, with a significant economy of time, when mathematics and science are integrated.
3. There is improved quality of learning and retention, supporting the thesis that learning which is meaningful and relevant is more effective.
4. Motivation and involvement are increased dramatically as students investigate real-world situations and participate actively in the process. We invite you to become part of this classroom teacher movement by using an integrated approach to learning and sharing any suggestions you may have. The AIMS Program welcomes you!

# AIMS Education Foundation Programs

## A Day with AIMS®

Intensive one-day workshops are offered to introduce educators to the philosophy and rationale of AIMS. Participants will discuss the methodology of AIMS and the strategies by which AIMS principles may be incorporated into curriculum. Each participant will take part in a variety of hands-on AIMS investigations to gain an understanding of such aspects as the scientific/mathematical content, classroom management, and connections with other curricular areas. *A Day with AIMS*® workshops may be offered anywhere in the United States. Necessary supplies and take-home materials are usually included in the enrollment fee.

## A Week with AIMS®

Throughout the nation, AIMS offers many one-week workshops each year, usually in the summer. Each workshop lasts five days and includes at least 30 hours of AIMS hands-on instruction. Participants are grouped according to the grade level(s) in which they are interested. Instructors are members of the AIMS Instructional Leadership Network. Supplies for the activities and a generous supply of take-home materials are included in the enrollment fee. Sites are selected on the basis of applications submitted by educational organizations. If chosen to host a workshop, the host agency agrees to provide specified facilities and cooperate in the promotion of the workshop. The AIMS Education Foundation supplies workshop materials as well as the travel, housing, and meals for instructors.

## AIMS One-Week Perspectives Workshops

Each summer, Fresno Pacific University offers AIMS one-week workshops on its campus in Fresno, California. AIMS Program Directors and highly qualified members of the AIMS National Leadership Network serve as instructors.

## The AIMS Instructional Leadership Program

This is an AIMS staff-development program seeking to prepare facilitators for leadership roles in science/math education in their home districts or regions. Upon successful completion of the program, trained facilitators may become members of the AIMS Instructional Leadership Network, qualified to conduct AIMS workshops, teach AIMS in-service courses for college credit, and serve as AIMS consultants. Intensive training is provided in mathematics, science, process and thinking skills, workshop management, and other relevant topics.

## College Credit and Grants

Those who participate in workshops may often qualify for college credit. If the workshop takes place on the campus of Fresno Pacific University, that institution may grant appropriate credit. If the workshop takes place off-campus, arrangements can sometimes be made for credit to be granted by another institution. In addition, the applicant's home school district is often willing to grant in-service or professional-development credit. Many educators who participate in AIMS workshops are recipients of various types of educational grants, either local or national. Nationally known foundations and funding agencies have long recognized the value of AIMS mathematics and science workshops to educators. The AIMS Education Foundation encourages educators interested in attending or hosting workshops to explore the possibilities suggested above. Although the Foundation strongly supports such interest, it reminds applicants that they have the primary responsibility for fulfilling *current* requirements.

**For current information regarding the programs described above, please complete the following:**

---

### *Information Request*

Please send current information on the items checked:

_____ *Basic Information Packet* on AIMS materials
_____ *AIMS Instructional Leadership Program*
_____ *AIMS One-Week Perspectives* workshops

_____ *A Week with AIMS*® workshops
_____ Hosting information for *A Day with AIMS*® workshops
_____ Hosting information for *A Week with AIMS*® workshops

Name_____ Phone_____

Address_____
       Street                                   City                            State     Zip

---

# We invite you to subscribe to AIMS!

Each issue of *AIMS* contains a variety of material useful to educators at all grade levels. Feature articles of lasting value deal with topics such as mathematical or science concepts, curriculum, assessment, the teaching of process skills, and historical background. Several of the latest AIMS math/science investigations are always included, along with their reproducible activity sheets. As needs direct and space allows, various issues contain news of current developments, such as workshop schedules, activities of the AIMS Instructional Leadership Network, and announcements of upcoming publications.

*AIMS* is published monthly, August through May. Subscriptions are on an annual basis only. A subscription entered at any time will begin with the next issue, but will also include the previous issues of that volume. Readers have preferred this arrangement because articles and activities within an annual volume are often interrelated.

Please note that an *AIMS* subscription automatically includes duplication rights for one school site for all issues included in the subscription. Many schools build cost-effective library resources with their subscriptions.

## YES! I am interested in subscribing to AIMS.

Name _____ Home Phone _____

Address _____ City, State, Zip _____

Please send the following volumes (subject to availability):

| | | | |
|---|---|---|---|
| _____ Volume VII (1992-93) $15.00 | _____ Volume XII (1997-98) $30.00 |
| _____ Volume VIII (1993-94) $15.00 | _____ Volume XIII (1998-99) $30.00 |
| _____ Volume IX (1994-95) $15.00 | _____ Volume XIV (1999-00) $30.00 |
| _____ Volume X (1995-96) $15.00 | _____ Volume XV (2000-01) $30.00 |
| _____ Volume XI (1996-97) $30.00 | _____ Volume XVI (2001-02) $30.00 |

_____ **Limited offer: Volumes XVI & XVII (2001-2003) $55.00**
(Note: Prices may change without notice)

**Check your method of payment:**

❑ Check enclosed in the amount of $ _____

❑ Purchase order attached (Please include the P.O.#, the authorizing signature, and position of the authorizing person.)

❑ Credit Card ❑ Visa ❑ MasterCard   Amount $ _____

Card # _____   Expiration Date _____

Signature _____   Today's Date _____

Make checks payable to **AIMS Education Foundation**.
Mail to *AIMS* Magazine, P.O. Box 8120, Fresno, CA 93747-8120.
Phone (559) 255-4094 or (888) 733-2467  FAX (559) 255-6396
**AIMS Homepage: http://www.AIMSedu.org/**

# AIMS Program Publications

## GRADES K-4 SERIES

Bats Incredible!
Brinca de Alegria Hacia la Primavera con las Matemáticas y Ciencias
Cáete de Gusto Hacia el Otoño con la Matemáticas y Ciencias
Cycles of Knowing and Growing
Fall Into Math and Science
Field Detectives
Glide Into Winter With Math and Science
Hardhatting in a Geo-World (Revised Edition, 1996)
Jaw Breakers and Heart Thumpers (Revised Edition, 1995)
Los Cincos Sentidos
Overhead and Underfoot  (Revised Edition, 1994)
Patine al Invierno con Matemáticas y Ciencias
Popping With Power (Revised Edition, 1996)
Primariamente Física (Revised Edition, 1994)
Primarily Earth
Primariamente Plantas
Primarily Physics (Revised Edition, 1994)
Primarily Plants
Sense-able Science
Spring Into Math and Science
Under Construction
Winter Wonders

## GRADES K-6 SERIES

Budding Botanist
Crazy About Cotton
Critters
El Botanista Principiante
Exploring Environments
Fabulous Fractions
Mostly Magnets
Ositos Nada Más
Primarily Bears
Principalmente Imanes
Water Precious Water

## GRADES 5-9 SERIES

Actions with Fractions
Brick Layers
Brick Layers II
Conexiones Eléctricas
Down to Earth
Electrical Connections
Finding Your Bearings (Revised Edition, 1996)
Floaters and Sinkers (Revised Edition, 1995)
From Head to Toe
Fun With Foods
Gravity Rules!
Historical Connections in Mathematics, Volume I
Historical Connections in Mathematics, Volume II
Historical Connections in Mathematics, Volume III
Just for the Fun of It!
Looking at Lines
Machine Shop
Magnificent Microworld Adventures
Math + Science, A Solution
Mutiplication the Algebra Way
Off the Wall Science: A Poster Series Revisited
Our Wonderful World
Out of This World  (Revised Edition, 1994)
Paper Square Geometry: The Mathematics of Origami
Pieces and Patterns, A Patchwork in Math and Science
Piezas y Diseños, un Mosaic de Matemáticas y Ciencias
Proportional Reasoning
Puzzle Play
Ray's Reflections
Soap Films and Bubbles
Spatial Visualization
The Sky's the Limit  (Revised Edition, 1994)
The Amazing Circle, Volume 1
Through the Eyes of the Explorers:
    Minds-on Math & Mapping
What's Next, Volume 1
What's Next, Volume 2
What's Next, Volume 3

For further information write to:

AIMS Education Foundation • P.O. Box 8120 • Fresno, California 93747-8120
www.AIMSedu.org/ • Fax 559•255•6396

# AIMS Duplication Rights Program

AIMS has received many requests from school districts for the purchase of unlimited duplication rights to AIMS materials. In response, the AIMS Education Foundation has formulated the program outlined below. There is a built-in flexibility which, we trust, will provide for those who use AIMS materials extensively to purchase such rights for either individual activities or entire books.

It is the goal of the AIMS Education Foundation to make its materials and programs available at reasonable cost. All income from the sale of publications and duplication rights is used to support AIMS programs; hence, strict adherence to regulations governing duplication is essential. Duplication of AIMS materials beyond limits set by copyright laws and those specified below is strictly forbidden.

### Limited Duplication Rights

Any purchaser of an AIMS book may make up to *200 copies* of any activity in that book for use at *one school site*. Beyond that, rights must be purchased according to the appropriate category.

### Unlimited Duplication Rights for Single Activities

An individual or school may purchase the right to make an unlimited number of copies of a single activity. The royalty is $5.00 per activity per school site.

Examples: 3 activities x 1 site  x $5.00 =  $15.00
9 activities x 3 sites x $5.00 = $135.00

### Unlimited Duplication Rights for Entire Books

A school or district may purchase the right to make an unlimited number of copies of a single, *specified* book. The royalty is $20.00 per book per school site. This is in addition to the cost of the book.

Examples: 5 books  x 1 site   x $20.00 = $100.00
12 books  x 10 sites x $20.00 = $2400.00

### Magazine/Newsletter Duplication Rights

Those who purchase *AIMS®* (magazine)/*Newsletter* are hereby granted permission to make up to 200 copies of any portion of it, provided these copies will be used for educational purposes.

### Workshop Instructors' Duplication Rights

Workshop instructors may distribute to registered workshop participants a maximum of 100 copies of any article and/or 100 copies of no more than eight activities, provided these six conditions are met:

1. Since all AIMS activities are based upon the *AIMS Model of Mathematics* and the *AIMS Model of Learning*, leaders must include in their presentations an explanation of these two models.
2. Workshop instructors must relate the AIMS activities presented to these basic explanations of the AIMS philosophy of education.
3. The copyright notice must appear on all materials distributed.
4. Instructors must provide information enabling participants to order books and magazines from the Foundation.
5. Instructors must inform participants of their limited duplication rights as outlined below.
6. Only student pages may be duplicated.

Written permission must be obtained for duplication beyond the limits listed above. Additional royalty payments may be required.

### Workshop Participants' Rights

Those enrolled in workshops in which AIMS student activity sheets are distributed may duplicate a maximum of 35 copies or enough to use the lessons one time with one class, whichever is less. Beyond that, rights must be purchased according to the appropriate category.

## Application for Duplication Rights

The purchasing agency or individual must clearly specify the following:
1. Name, address, and telephone number
2. Titles of the books for Unlimited Duplication Rights contracts
3. Titles of activities for Unlimited Duplication Rights contracts
4. Names and addresses of school sites for which duplication rights are being purchased.

*NOTE: Books to be duplicated must be purchased separately and are not included in the contract for Unlimited Duplication Rights.*

The requested duplication rights are automatically authorized when proper payment is received, although a *Certificate of Duplication Rights* will be issued when the application is processed.

Address all correspondence to:  **Contract Division**
**AIMS Education Foundation**
P.O. Box 8120
Fresno, CA  93747-8120

www.AIMSedu.org/
Fax 559•255•6396